MARY

DEVOTED TO GOD'S PLAN

Also available in the Studies in Faithful Living Series

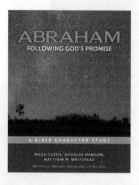

Abraham: Following God's Promise

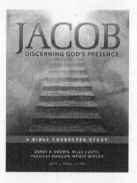

Jacob: Discerning God's Presence

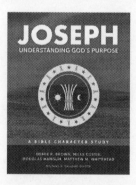

Joseph: Understanding God's Purpose

For updates on this series, visit LexhamPress.com/SFL

MARY

DEVOTED TO GOD'S PLAN

Studies in Faithful Living

Miles Custis
Douglas Mangum
Matthew M. Whitehead
Rebecca Brant
John D. Barry
Elizabeth Vince

Editor

Michael R. Grigoni

LEXHAM PRESS

Mary: Devoted to God's Plan
Studies in Faithful Living

Copyright 2014 Lexham Press

Lexham Press, 1313 Commercial St., Bellingham, WA 98225
LexhamPress.com

ISBN 978-1-57-799579-1

Assistant Editor: Jennifer Hendrix
Cover Design: Jim LePage
Typesetting: ProjectLuz.com

TABLE OF CONTENTS

Introduction vii

1. Embracing the Unexpected 1

2. Exceptional Praise 12

3. A Unique Birth 24

4. A Foretelling of Sacrifice 35

5. Facing Fear with Faith 47

6. Preparing to Let Go 60

7. Family Redefined 71

8. Behold Your Son 82

Conclusion 93

Notes 95

Sources 98

About the Editor and Authors 101

INTRODUCTION

The story of Mary's life opens with a shocking event: Without warning or invitation, the angel Gabriel suddenly appears to Mary and announces that she will be the mother of Jesus (Luke 1:26–33). Mary responds with "let it be to me according to your word" (Luke 1:38) Thus begins the dramatic story of Mary, mother of Jesus. While the subsequent steps of her journey do not get easier—imagine raising the Son of God!—her story teaches us a profound lesson: the life of faith is made up of a series of steps that bring us closer to the fulfillment of God's will, but not necessarily farther from the challenges and struggles involved with moving ahead.

Looking at the "steps" that make up the lives of people like Mary is one way to engage with the story of the Bible. This is the approach taken by the Studies in Faithful Living series. In this volume, we examine the life of an ordinary young woman who received an extraordinary call from God, drawing out the lessons her faithful response provides for us. Studying the Bible in this way teaches us to model the exceptional characters of Scripture and grow in our efforts to imitate Christ. In doing so, we enter deeper into the story the Bible narrates for us: God's redemption of creation—a story that continues in the lives of those who respond to him today.

We begin in Chapter 1 by considering Gabriel's announcement to Mary and her assent to God's plan. In Chapter 2, we journey with Mary to visit Elizabeth and hear the words of the *Magnificat*, Mary's outpouring of praise to God for choosing her to give birth to the Messiah. Chapter 3 relates Mary and Joseph's trek to Bethlehem and the humble yet wondrous circumstances of Jesus' birth. In Chapter 4, we follow Mary and Joseph as they present Jesus in the temple and learn more about his significance through Simeon and Anna. Chapter 5 considers the visitation by the magi and Herod's threat to kill the Christ-child. In Chapter 6, we find Mary frantically searching for Jesus, who stayed behind in the temple during Passover. Chapter 7 considers two events: Mary's prompting Jesus at a wedding in Cana and Jesus' new definition of family as "whoever does the will of God" (Mark 3:35). Chapter 8 brings us to the foot of the cross, where Mary watches her Son die. Throughout the study, we witness Mary's steadfast devotion to God's plan as she grows into an understanding of her Son's purpose and mission.

To help you dig deeper into these biblical accounts, we've arranged each chapter into five sections. In *Setting the Stage*, we introduce the theme of the chapter and the significant literary, historical, and cultural details of the story at hand. *A Closer Look* illuminates the narrative by walking you through the story itself. *Throughout the Bible* connects the Old and New Testaments and shows how the biblical authors have understood the story under consideration at various points in biblical history. *Beyond the Bible* accomplishes a similar task by exploring the story within various historical contexts. This leads to the *Application*, where we discuss the relevance of Mary's experiences for our lives today. Application and reflection questions conclude each chapter to help you contemplate and internalize what you've learned.

Ultimately, the underlying theme of Mary's story isn't that different from ours. In agreeing to Gabriel's announcement, Mary responded faithfully to God's call and began an extraordinary journey—one that led her not only to becoming the mother of Jesus, but also to becoming his disciple. Her unyielding devotion to God's plan resulted in her transformation into what God desires for all of us: to become followers of his Son. May this study aid you in your pursuit of God's will and bring you closer to the completion of the work God is faithfully performing in your life (Phil 1:6).

CHAPTER 1

EMBRACING THE UNEXPECTED

Read Luke 1:26–38 and Matthew 1:18–25.

SETTING THE STAGE

Theme. If we've followed God for any length of time, we know to expect difficulties and challenges in life. They are one way he helps us grow. Sometimes God asks us to do things that seem outrageous or extreme, or he leads us into demanding circumstances because he wants to use us in them. But when God unexpectedly asks us to step out in a way that jeopardizes our comfort or our life, we often resist—even when we realize he's asking us to play a role in his plan.

It's hard to imagine God making any request more extreme than what he asked of Mary. As she went about what would have been an ordinary day, God dispatched Gabriel, his divine messenger, to announce that he had chosen her to give birth to his own Son. In spite of the bewilderment of this divine encounter, Mary remained composed and responded with humility, surrender, and praise. She must have known she would face public shame and scorn from her small, close-knit community. But even without knowing all the details, she devoted herself completely to God's plan, saying "Behold, I am the servant of the Lord; let it be to me according to your word" (Luke 1:38 ESV).

Literary Context. Luke opens his Gospel by announcing that "I too decided ... to write an orderly account for you, most excellent Theophilus, so that you may know the truth concerning the things about which you have been instructed" (Luke 1:3-4). This orderly account begins with the birth announcements of John the Baptist and Jesus. By introducing his Gospel in this way, Luke sets the stage for Mary's profound assent to God's will.

> **Quick Bit:** In Jewish literature, Gabriel is one of the seven arch-angels—the highest angelic order—that function as God's princes or vice regents. He appears as a messenger in both Luke and Daniel. His presence signifies both the importance of his message and God's favor toward the recipient (Dan 8:15-17; 9:21-23; Luke 1:19, 26-33). Only Daniel, Zechariah, and Mary are said to have conversed with Gabriel which shows God's high regard for these individuals (Dan 9:23; Luke 1:28).

Luke first records the angel Gabriel's appearance to Elizabeth and Zechariah and his announcement that they would have a son, John (see Luke 1:5-25). In the verses immediately following, Luke records Gabriel's visitation to Mary, proclaiming she would give birth to a son, Jesus (Luke 1:26-38). The pairing of these accounts draws our attention to their similarities and differences, foreshadowing the relationship between John and Jesus in their ministries. In each case, God sent Gabriel to announce the birth (Luke 1:19, 26-28). The angel told the future parents what to name their sons and foretold the profound influence their sons would have (Luke 1:13-17, 31-33). And in both instances, the recipients of the unexpected message questioned Gabriel, who described the events to come as evidence of God's power (Luke 1:18-20, 34-37).

What makes these announcements different are the recipients' life circumstances. Zechariah was a priest serving God in the temple when Gabriel appeared to him. He and his wife, Elizabeth, were old and had no children (see Luke 1:7). We can presume that the couple wished for a child and even prayed that God would give them one. For Zechariah and Elizabeth, Gabriel's news was cause for great celebration.[1]

In contrast, Mary was just a young girl. She was betrothed to Joseph but not married to him. In Mary's culture an unwed woman getting pregnant was not only shameful, it also violated biblical law. Gabriel's message to Mary was cause for great anxiety. He prefaced his announcement by saying, "Do not be afraid" (Luke 1:30), but how could any girl not be afraid? How could Mary explain this pregnancy to her family and to Joseph, her betrothed? Who would believe her? Would she be cast out of her village? Would she be stoned? Yet rather than allowing fear to overcome her, Mary displayed great courage and faith as she humbly embraced her role as "the servant of the Lord" (Luke 1:38 ESV).

Historical & Cultural Background. Luke reveals two key details about Mary: She was a virgin, and she was engaged to marry Joseph (Luke 1:27). These facts alone reveal the serious situation to which Mary surrendered herself, body and spirit. Unlike modern engagements, Mary's betrothal to Joseph was a legally binding arrangement. Betrothals, the first stage of the marriage process in the ancient Near East, were initiated by the parents of the groom, who paid a "bride price" to the woman's family.[2] Women could be betrothed as young as 12 years old. The second stage of the process, the marriage itself, usually took place about a year after the betrothal.

In many respects, betrothal in Mary's day carried a weight equal to marriage. As a legally binding arrangement, a betrothal could be broken only by divorce. Even before marriage, the betrothed couple would often be referred to as husband and wife (see Matt 1:19, which calls Joseph "[Mary's] husband"). And most significant for Mary's situation, any sexual infidelity during the betrothal period was considered adultery and was punishable by death under the Mosaic law (see Deut 22:23–24).

Mary had every reason to feel anxious over Gabriel's announcement. Her pregnancy placed her on a path of family shame and community scorn, and it put her very life in danger. When we understand what was at stake for Mary, her calm, courageous surrender to God's will becomes even more profound.

A CLOSER LOOK

Imagine what it must have been like for Mary. At the time of Gabriel's announcement, she is living an ordinary life. Although we don't know her exact age, we can assume that Mary is in her early to mid-teens since she is engaged but not yet married. Mary undoubtedly still lives with her parents in Nazareth, a small village in rural Galilee. The day of Gabriel's announcement must have started out like any other. But when Gabriel bursts into her life with miraculous news, we begin to see the remarkable depths of her faith.

> **Quick Bit:** Luke uses the Greek verb *ginōskō*, meaning "to know," to express the common OT Hebrew euphemism for sexual relations (Luke 1:34). This practice may reflect the influence of the OT on biblical Greek since this euphemism is less common in Greek literature. Many English translations render Mary's statement in Luke 1:34 with similar expressions that clarify the sexual connotation intended here.

Gabriel greets Mary by declaring that she is highly favored by God (Luke 1:28). While Mary works through her bewilderment over the angel's greeting (not to mention his stunning appearance in her home), Gabriel delivers his divine pronouncement: God has chosen her to give birth to his Son, the long-awaited Messiah of Israel (Luke 1:29–33).

Gabriel's announcement paints a regal portrait of the holy child's future: He will be named Jesus. He will be called the "Son of the Most High" and the "Son of God." He will possess the "throne of his father David" and rule over Israel forever (Luke 1:31–35). Gabriel reveals that the birth of this child is the fulfillment of OT prophecy pointing to the coming of the Messiah (see "Throughout the Bible"). When Mary interrupts Gabriel, however, the question she poses is utterly practical: How could she, a virgin, become pregnant? The only obstacle Mary sees to the plan is the fact that she has not "known" a man.

Telling Mary that the miraculous power of God will enable her pregnancy, Gabriel also delivers the news of Elizabeth's extraordinary pregnancy as confirmation of all that he's told her (Luke 1:36–37). Her question answered, Mary accepts her role in God's plan.

Luke's narrative doesn't provide much detail about the aftermath of Mary's decision: She spends her first trimester with her relative Elizabeth, the only mother-to-be who could identify with and understand her astounding story (Luke 1:56). Mary could not hide her pregnancy from her family, but we never learn their reaction to her explanation of the conception.

The Gospel of Matthew gives us a glimpse into Joseph's reaction (Matt 1:18–25). Joseph is clearly upset when he learns Mary is pregnant.

He decides to break their engagement quietly to avoid disgracing her publicly, indicating the news hadn't spread much outside the immediate family. Since breaking a betrothal was a legal action—essentially a formal divorce (see "Setting the Stage")—Joseph is obviously not convinced by Mary's explanation that she is pregnant "by the Holy Spirit" (Matt 1:18).

To reassure Joseph that Mary hadn't been unfaithful, God sends an angel in a dream to confirm Mary's explanation. The angel declares that Joseph should proceed with the marriage and confirms that the pregnancy originated with God himself. Joseph also learns that the child is to be named "Jesus" because he will grow up to "save his people from their sins" (Matt 1:21). The dream convinces Joseph that Mary's amazing story is true, and he follows through by marrying her. Just as Luke takes pains to emphasize Mary's virginity, Matthew explicitly states that Joseph "did not know" her before she gave birth to Jesus (Matt 1:25).

Mary's acceptance of God's plan radically changes her life and puts her entire future in jeopardy. Joseph could have broken off the marriage arrangement, and if Mary's status as an unwed mother became widely known, she would have been subjected to public shame, ridicule, or even death. Being pregnant outside of wedlock would have created insurmountable obstacles to any future marriage possibilities. The Bible doesn't say whether Mary considers these threats to her future before surrendering to God's will. She simply recognizes that the only action she needs to take is to obey.

THROUGHOUT THE BIBLE

The announcements of Jesus' birth in the Gospels of Luke and Matthew make many references to OT prophecies about the coming Messiah. A key verse Matthew and Luke both draw on is the Septuagint version of Isaiah 7:14: "Behold, a virgin will conceive and will bear a son, and you will call his name Immanuel." The Greek word used in this verse, *parthenos*, is usually translated as "virgin" and refers to a young, unmarried woman who would most likely have been chaste. This same word is used in Luke 1:27 and Matthew 1:23. Taken with the fact that "Immanuel" means "God with us," Luke and Matthew both understood the Septuagint of Isaiah 7:14 as pointing to Jesus' birth.

While Matthew explicitly quotes Isaiah 7:14 (see Matt 1:23), Luke merely alludes to this prophecy. He does so by referring to Mary as the "virgin," or *parthenos*, twice in Luke 1:27. Mary's words in Luke 1:34 likewise confirm her having been sexually chaste. Even though Luke doesn't explicitly cite the OT reference, he undoubtedly has Isaiah 7:14 LXX in mind.

Luke's subtle allusion prepares readers for what is to come. Even if Mary was shocked at the news, readers would realize that Gabriel's pronouncement aligned perfectly with what the OT told them to expect. In his Gospel, Matthew makes his understanding of Isaiah 7:14 very clear by stating, "Now all this happened in order that what was spoken by the Lord through the prophet would be fulfilled" (Matt 1:22). Matthew's quotation explicitly indicates the prophetic origin of Mary's role and emphasizes that Jesus is the long-expected "Immanuel."

> **Quick Bit:** The Septuagint (also known as the LXX) is a Greek translation of the Hebrew Bible. It most likely originated during the third to second century BC to give Greek-speaking Jews a translation of their scriptures during the Hellenistic period. It is especially relevant for NT study because NT writers, who wrote in Greek, drew from the Septuagint as their primary version of Scripture.

In the Gospel of Luke, the messianic allusions extend far deeper than Isaiah 7:14. Gabriel tells Mary that her child will be the "Son of the Most High" who will sit on the "throne of his father David" and "reign over the house of Jacob forever" (Luke 1:32–33). The title "Most High" emphasizes God's transcendence and may also have evoked a connection with the priest Melchizedek (Gen 14:18–22), who would later be used to illustrate Jesus' own priesthood (Heb 7:1). Elsewhere, Luke refers to Jesus as "Son of the Most High God" (Luke 8:28), a title that alludes to Jesus' divine origin by drawing on OT traditions about other heavenly beings (Psa 82:6).

Luke's account of Gabriel's message also draws on language from God's covenant with David that would have been even more familiar to readers of his Gospel. In 2 Samuel 7:12–16, God promises David that his royal dynasty will "endure forever," and his "throne" will "be established forever" (2 Sam 7:16). Later biblical writers rooted their messianic hopes in this promise to David, and the prophets predicted a ruler from the line of David who would fulfill this hope (Isa 9:7; Jer 33:17–21). Mary was likely familiar with these prophecies and would have understood Gabriel's meaning: The time of fulfillment was soon, and her son was the promised ruler who would restore Israel. But like many people of that time, Mary probably expected the Messiah to free them from Rome and establish his kingdom on earth. As one of Jesus' early followers, she would only gradually come to realize that his mission and plan would take a completely unexpected course.

BEYOND THE BIBLE

If Mary was stunned by Gabriel's revelation of her baby's destiny (Luke 1:31–33), she didn't show it. For her the most critical detail of the angel's announcement was the most practical, the one thing she might have had control over: how she, a virgin, could possibly conceive a child (Luke 1:34). Mary was the first in countless generations to wonder how this impossible event would come to be. Yet this is how God chose to bring his Son, Jesus, into the world.

This miracle has been a source of amazement and inspiration for millions of people for the last 2,000 years. Countless artists and poets have attempted to capture the awe and mystery of the divine conception—in words, paint, marble, even stained glass. Mary voiced her wonder and amazement in the words of the *Magnificat*, a touchstone depiction of this unprecedented event (Luke 1:46–55). Some of the most beautiful reflections have come from people outside the Bible. Prudentius, a Latin poet, hymn writer, and apologist (ca. AD 348–410), expressed his amazement at God's power and creativity in Mary's miraculous conception:

> By power of God a spotless maid conceives,
> As in her virgin womb the Spirit breathes.
> The mystery of this birth confirms our faith
> That Christ is God: a maiden by the Spirit
> Is wed, unstained by love; her purity
> Remains intact; with child within, untouched
> Without, bright in her chaste fertility,
> Mother yet virgin, mother that knew not man.[3]

Prudentius' eloquent words highlight key themes from Luke's account. By the Spirit's "breath," God caused the virgin, Mary, to conceive. "That Christ is God" echoes the identity of Mary's child as "Son of the Most High" (Luke 1:32). God's power caused a virgin to conceive—a miraculous act reserved for God's Son alone. Prudentius scoffed at those who refused to believe the angel's words:

> Why, doubter, do you shake your silly head?
> An angel makes this known with holy lips.
> Will you not hearken to angelic words?[4]

Read alongside Luke's account, Prudentius' poem underscores the devotion Mary exhibited in response to Gabriel's explanation of the divine conception (Luke 1:35-37). Like Prudentius centuries later, Mary embraced the angel's revelation and marveled at God's unparalleled provision. No matter the personal sacrifice involved, Mary embraced God's plan and devoted herself to it, realizing its significance for his people (see Luke 1:54). We, too, can marvel at God's unique intervention in history and its eternal impact: The Messiah, born of a virgin, brought salvation to the world.

APPLICATION

When things are going well in our lives, we can easily slip into a spiritual lull. God blends into the busy background of our days, the all-but-invisible divine safety net if trouble should arise. But when we look at where God is at work—in our lives, in the world—there's hardly a smooth road in sight. God calls us to grow and to participate in his plan. And that can mean allowing him to use us in ways we never imagined.

Mary would have never expected to play such an important role in God's plan. The Gospels give us very few details about Mary—only that she was a young virgin, living in a small town and betrothed to a man named Joseph. But through her response to God's extreme call, we learn much more about her than the superficial facts.

As any of us would be, Mary was scared. Luke tells us she was "greatly troubled" (Luke 1:29) at Gabriel's announcement. But she didn't panic. In

the overwhelming presence of a divine messenger, Mary composed herself and listened to the angel's pronouncement. We know from other passages that Mary often pondered the things going on around her (Luke 2:19,
51), so she probably wondered what would become of her future—her
reputation, her betrothal, even her life. In spite of the obvious danger she
faced by taking on this role in God's plan, she humbly and courageously
surrendered herself—body and spirit—saying, "Behold, I am the servant
of the Lord; let it be to me according to your word" (Luke 1:38 ESV). And
she responded not only with obedience, but also with praise.

When called to step out onto the path of extraordinary faith, Mary
showed herself to be levelheaded, attentive, and courageous. In accepting
the unique blessing God offered her, she put aside her life, surrendered
her body, and expressed utter faith and obedience. When we face struggles in our lives—or when we encounter blessings that come at a high
price—we need look no further than Mary to find an exceptional model
of faith.

DISCUSSION

A Closer Look

1. Reflect on a time when you felt stuck between obeying God and doing the "right" thing in the eyes of your family and friends. How was your response like or unlike Mary's?

_____

_____

_____

2. Mary's "yes" to God radically changed any plans she may have had for her own life. Think about how your life would change if God called you to make a radical choice to serve him (like becoming a missionary in a far-off country or starting full-time ministry).

_____

_____

_____

Throughout the Bible

1. Reflect on a similar experience in your own life: When has God's plan for you overturned your expectations?

_____

_____

2. Read through some of the ot references expressing hope in the coming Messiah, such as Isaiah 9:2–7; Jeremiah 33:14–26. How do these passages help you understand what Mary was expecting?

_____

_____

_____

Beyond the Bible

1. What is the significance of a virgin conceiving a child? What does it say about the identity of Jesus' Father, as well as his own identity?

_____

_____

_____

2. How can Mary's response to difficult and unexpected news serve as an example in your life?

_____

_____

_____

Application

1. Has God ever asked you to do something that scared you? How did you respond? If he asks you to act in extreme faith, how can you overcome your fear?

_____

_____

_____

2. Think of a time you experienced growth in your spiritual life. Were your circumstances comfortable? Were they challenging? How did you respond?

_____

_____

_____

CHAPTER 2

EXCEPTIONAL PRAISE

Read Luke 1:39–56.

SETTING THE STAGE

Theme. As believers, we all have a divine appointment—a particular role to fill in God's plan. Sometimes we struggle to discern what God is calling us to do, or we wonder whether we correctly understand his will. At other times we have absolute conviction about our mission in life. When we do, it's probably because God has used people and circumstances in our lives to clarify or confirm his will for us, as we see in Mary's story. When he provides that confirmation, we need to humbly surrender our desires for the sake of accomplishing what he desires.

Few people in the Bible model this behavior better than Mary. Upon learning her role in God's plan, Mary likely needed confirmation about her experience. So she traveled to visit her relative, Elizabeth, who confirmed that God had indeed chosen Mary to fulfill his great purpose. Hearing these words from a trusted friend who understood the nature of a miraculous pregnancy, Mary responded with exultation and humble surrender to God's will, devoting her body and her baby to God's plan of redemption. Mary emptied herself of personal goals and desires to become a vessel to be used by God for his purposes.

Literary Context. Luke's description of Mary leaving to see Elizabeth directly follows Gabriel's revelation that both she and Elizabeth would have children. Luke tells us that Elizabeth was already six months pregnant when Gabriel announced to Mary that God had chosen her to have his Son (Luke 1:26). The phrase "in those days" along with the note that Mary "traveled with haste" (Luke 1:39) suggests that Mary departed immediately to visit Elizabeth.

Mary might have had any number of reasons for wanting to see Elizabeth. It's natural to think Mary wanted to hide her pregnancy. After all, it put her life at risk since adultery was punishable by death according to Mosaic law (see Deut 22:23-24; see also Chapter 1). But Mary remained with Elizabeth for only three months; she returned home before the birth of John and just when her own pregnancy would be beginning to show (see Luke 1:56-57).

More likely, Mary visited Elizabeth because of Gabriel's announcement. When Mary asked the archangel how she—as a virgin—could possibly conceive, Gabriel declared, "Nothing will be impossible with God" (Luke 1:37). He had just revealed to Mary that Elizabeth had conceived a son despite her barrenness and age (see Luke 1:34-36), as if offering Elizabeth's situation as proof. Mary was eager to see Elizabeth with her own eyes and behold the miracle Gabriel gave as the confirmation of his message.

If Mary visited Elizabeth seeking evidence of God's power, she certainly found it. The sight of Elizabeth, swollen in her sixth month of pregnancy, confirmed Gabriel's proclamation. What's more, Mary gained certainty about her own role in God's plan through Elizabeth's exclamation after she was filled with the Holy Spirit. Bolstered by such divine reassurance, Mary spontaneously responded by singing praise to God.

Historical & Cultural Background. Luke does not tell us exactly where Elizabeth lived in Judah. He simply describes the area as "the hill country" (Luke 1:39). The book of Joshua lists nine cities in the hill country of the tribe of Judah (Josh 15:48-54; see also Josh 11:21). It's likely Elizabeth and Zechariah lived in the hilly region to the southwest of Jerusalem.

Mary came from Nazareth, a Galilean city west of the Sea of Galilee (see Luke 1:26). Her journey from Nazareth to the hill country of Judah covered between 80 and 100 miles. Luke does not mention whether Mary made any preparations for the trip or how she traveled; she may have gone on foot or as part of a caravan. In Mary's day, a person traveling by foot could cover about 20 miles per day. If Mary walked to Elizabeth's home, it would have taken her four to five days.[1] If she accompanied a caravan, she would have arrived in about three days.

In either case, Mary demonstrated her courage as well as her desire for confirmation of God's plan—such a journey would have been dangerous, especially for a young girl alone. Mary serves as a role model, not only for her obedience, but for her action. She allowed her devotion to overcome any fear she may have had about surrendering to God's call on her life or any danger she may have faced in confirming his will. Such complete surrender freed her to act in confidence.

A CLOSER LOOK

In Luke's Gospel, Mary arrives on Elizabeth's doorstep unexpectedly. Elizabeth would have no reason to anticipate Mary's visit; in fact, the idea of a young, unmarried woman traveling more than 80 miles alone was unheard of in Mary's day. But Elizabeth shows no surprise when Mary calls out in greeting, and at the sound of her voice, Elizabeth rejoices at the great privilege that God has given both of them—to Mary, that she would bear God's own Son; to her, that she should see the mother of her Savior and find fulfillment of her faith in God's promises.

> **Quick Bit:** Luke uses a relatively rare Greek word (*skirtaō*) to describe how Elizabeth's baby "leap[s]" at the sound of Mary's voice. The verb appears only three times in the NT: twice in this passage and once in Luke 6 (Luke 1:41, 44; 6:23). In using this rare word, Luke likely intends to echo the Septuagint version of Genesis 25:22, which uses the verb to describe the movement of Esau and Jacob in Rebecca's womb.

We don't know what Mary says when she greets Elizabeth, since Luke's Gospel contains only Elizabeth's words. Luke structures his narrative to emphasize Elizabeth's response, suggesting Mary's greeting may be nothing more than "hello." But the mere sound of Mary's voice rouses Elizabeth's unborn son, John, who "leap[s]" in his mother's womb (Luke 1:41).

Elizabeth understands her baby's movement is a prophetic sign of the importance of her visitor. According to cultural norms, Mary should show respect for Elizabeth as an older woman and the wife of a priest; Mary conducts herself accordingly when she enters Elizabeth's home and greets her.[2] In response to her baby's stirring, Elizabeth turns the tables, greeting Mary with the respect due her for her not-yet-realized superiority. In pronouncing Mary "blessed," Elizabeth casts Mary as the superior (Luke 1:42).

John's movement in his mother's womb also marks the beginning of his ministry to proclaim the coming of the Messiah (Luke 1:15–17). Mary and Elizabeth's interaction also serves to foreshadow the coming relationship between John and Jesus. In both cases, the older recognizes the superiority of the younger.

Since Mary has not revealed her situation to Elizabeth, she would have been quite surprised to hear Elizabeth exclaim that she is "blessed." This pronouncement echoes OT affirmations of divinely empowered women such as Jael (Judg 5:24) as well as Gabriel's statement that Mary is the "favored one" (Luke 1:28). Elizabeth testifies to the divine origin of Mary's pregnancy, pronouncing a blessing on the unborn child and expressing surprise at the unexpected visit from "the mother of my Lord" (Luke 1:43). Although Mary visits Elizabeth to find confirmation of Gabriel's words about Elizabeth's pregnancy, she also finds confirmation of the archangel's announcement that she herself would conceive. Both women find blessing in companionship: Elizabeth, who has "kept herself hidden" for the five months since she conceived (Luke 1:24), no doubt took great comfort in Mary's visit. And Mary could lean on Elizabeth's understanding of the immense blessing, and inherent loneliness, of being set apart for God's purpose. Elizabeth further serves as a prophetess, speaking by the Holy Spirit to confirm God's calling on Mary's life (Luke 1:41).

Just as Mary's voice rouses John to leap in Elizabeth's womb, so Elizabeth's blessing on Mary evokes an immediate outpouring of praise. Her song of exultation has become a hymn traditionally called the *Magnificat* (from the first word of the hymn in the Latin Vulgate). Mary's song is much more than an expression of humility and obedience to God. Its structure and themes are often compared to OT poetry, especially Hannah's song from 1 Samuel 2 (see "Throughout the Bible").

Mary's song introduces themes of salvation and redemption that Luke interweaves throughout his Gospel, drawing heavily on OT imagery of God's interactions with Israel. In doing so, the *Magnificat* interrupts the narrative and creates a pause to reflect on all God has done for his people. At the same time, the song represents Mary's expression of her deeper understanding and ongoing acceptance of God's plan and her role in that plan. Her words celebrate the story of God's redemption, presenting the astonishing events she has just experienced and the long-expected fulfillment of God's promise of a Messiah.[3]

Mary's hymn resembles the structure of OT praise psalms, which often open with the psalmist exalting God and then listing the many reasons God is worthy of all praise. Mary begins her hymn with an outpouring of her heartfelt praise, singing, "My soul exalts the Lord, and my spirit has rejoiced greatly in God my Savior" (Luke 1:46-7). She recognizes and openly acknowledges that God has blessed her with a central role in his plan of salvation—even though she is a young woman with no social status (Luke 1:48).

Mary refers to herself as the Lord's "female slave" (Luke 1:48) just as she did in her reply to Gabriel in Luke 1:38. The Greek word *doulē* (like the masculine form *doulos*) expresses an attitude of humility and obedience. English translations render the word as "servant" or "slave." Although the term was used to denote the literal meaning of slave in terms of the relationship between slave and master, it was also frequently used by those of lower status to refer to themselves when addressing their superiors. Mary uses the word to express her respect and deference, humbly acknowledging that God has blessed her by giving her a central role in his plan.

Having recognizing God's particular care for her, Mary turns her praise to his attributes. She declares him mighty and sings "holy is his name" (Luke 1:49). In biblical times, referring to a person's name indicated reputation or character (see Prov 22:1). By proclaiming that God's name is holy, Mary says God himself is holy. Mary also lauds God's mercy, noting that it continues "for generation after generation to those who fear him" (Luke 1:50).

Mary expands her hymn of tribute to praise God for bringing the proud low while exalting the humble (Luke 1:51-2). The theme of God protecting the lowly or needy while punishing the arrogant or oppressive runs throughout the OT (see Psa 107:40-41; Prov 3:34; 15:25). Mary continues in this vein by singing God's glory for "[filling] the hungry with good things, and [sending] the rich away empty" (Luke 1:53 NRSV).

Mary then turns her song to praise God for his ongoing care and compassion specifically for Israel. She testifies that God has helped Israel by "remembering his mercy, just as he spoke to our fathers, to Abraham and to his descendants forever" (Luke 1:54-5). Mary beautifully unites past and future by interweaving God's promise to Abraham—to bless his descendants and go on to bless the world through him (Gen 12:1-3)—with the birth of Jesus. Despite her youth, Mary demonstrates a mature understanding of Scripture in her hymn. Her praise also proclaims her unwavering willingness to cast off her own wants, desires, and plans to accept her role in God's great plan to redeem.

THROUGHOUT THE BIBLE

The themes of Mary's *Magnificat* reflect those of Hannah's song in 1 Samuel 2:1-10. Hannah was married to a man who had another wife—one who had given him children (1 Sam 1:1-2). Although her husband loved her, Hannah was relentlessly taunted by the other wife for being barren (1 Sam 1:6). When God answered her prayer for a son (Samuel), Hannah rejoiced by exalting God's goodness and provision (1 Sam 1:20). Although Mary and Hannah were in very different situations, both women praised God for remembering the desperate plight of his people.

In rewarding Hannah by providing her with Samuel, God also satisfied Israel's need for a great leader—something the nation lacked since the death of Moses (Deut 34). As God's prophet, Samuel would bring Israel out of spiritual darkness and back into a proper relationship with him (1 Sam 7:3-6). Israel also lacked a great leader in Mary's time. Yet Mary's son would accomplish far more than the salvation of Israel, just as Gabriel proclaimed (Luke 1:31-33). Mary's son was born to fulfill God's plan to save his people from their sins (Matt 1:21).

Quick Bit: The Jews in Mary's day eagerly anticipated the coming of a messiah. They longed for him to set them free from the Romans' imposed rule, purify temple worship, and establish a just utopian society: the kingdom of God. The birth of Jesus, as predicted by Gabriel, offered hope in the midst of darkness, much like Samuel's birth in 1 Samuel 1–2.

Both mothers knew that their sons—Samuel and Jesus–were destined for greatness, and they expressed their thanksgiving to God with songs of praise. Both songs open by praising God for revealing his salvation. Hannah's song declares "I rejoice in your salvation" (1 Sam 2:1), while Mary sings that her spirit "rejoices in God my Savior" (Luke 1:47). The praises reflect the source of their joy and strength: God himself. Both songs elevate God's holiness, with Hannah exclaiming that "there is none holy like the Lord" (1 Sam 2:2) and Mary rejoicing "holy is his name" (Luke 1:49).

Hannah and Mary both describe God as a God of action. They extol his sovereignty and the strength by which he elevates the humble and needy (1 Sam 2:7–8; Luke 1:48) and abolishes the proud (1 Sam 2:3; Luke 1:51). Mary testifies that God has "done great things" for her personally (Luke 1:49) and shown his mercy to his people "from generation to generation" (Luke 1:50). Hannah declares "The Lord makes poor and makes rich" (1 Sam 2:7). She describes him as a God who defeats his enemies and guards his people (1 Sam 2:9–10).

Each woman's song concludes with hints of coming salvation. Hannah proclaims that God will "exalt the horn of his anointed (or Messiah)" (1 Sam 2:10). Hannah's son, Samuel, helped pave the way for the Messiah by anointing David as king of Israel (see 1 Sam 16:1–13)—the king from whom Jesus would descend (see Matt 1:1–17). Hannah's song ultimately points beyond her son to Mary's.

Through both Hannah and Mary, God sovereignly intervened to save his people. In Mary's elegant *Magnificat,* she identified her situation with God's great redemptive work of the past—namely what he had accomplished through Hannah and Samuel. Through her song, Mary also gave new voice to her willingness to embrace her role in God's plan.

BEYOND THE BIBLE

Mary was willing to give everything to accomplish God's will. Although the circumstances of her pregnancy put her in danger of scorn, abandonment, and even death, Mary embraced God's plan for her life because she knew it would ultimately benefit all people (Luke 1:31–33, 38). Being chosen by God to give birth to the Messiah was an exceptional honor, one she sang about with wonder in her *Magnificat*: "from now on all generations will consider me blessed" (Luke 1:48).

Despite this realization, Mary deflected praise to the One who granted her this immense privilege. Although she recognized she would always be honored as the woman who gave birth to the Messiah, Mary knew the highest honor belonged to God for his salvation (Luke 1:54). But in spite of Mary's efforts to direct praise to God's redemptive work, some early Christians focused on her instead. They developed legends to extol the significance of her role.

> **Quick Bit:** The *Protevangelium of James* is an apocryphal gospel—a collection of nonbiblical legends—that expands on the birth narratives of Matthew and Luke. Allegedly written by Jesus' half-brother, James, this apocryphal gospel was actually composed in the second century AD. Its legends reflect early Christian curiosity about the circumstances surrounding Jesus' birth and attempt to answer questions the Bible does not address. By studying ancient documents like this one, we can gain a better understanding of the early church and the way it understood the Bible.

One collection of these legends, the *Protevangelium of James*, records a series of prophecies concerning Mary's future honor. The first prophecy was made to Mary's barren mother. The story is similar to Hannah's in 1 Samuel 1–2. After Mary's mother prayed for a child, an angel appeared to her and announced that she would give birth to a great child: "Your offspring will be spoken of throughout the whole world."[4] Following Mary's birth, various priests continued to make similar prophetic announcements. On Mary's first birthday, a priest asked God to give her "a name renowned forever among all generations." And when she turned three, another priest blessed Mary by declaring that "The Lord has magnified your name among all generations." A third priest confirmed these predictions following the annunciation: "Mary, the Lord God has magnified your name, and you will be blessed among all generations of the earth!"

But the *Protevangelium of James* comes full circle. Despite its emphasis on Mary's greatness, its author eventually recognizes the greatness of God's redemption *through* the role Mary played in God's plan. The priest who blessed her on her third birthday also predicted, "In the future, the Lord will manifest his redemption through you to the children of Israel." Following the birth of Jesus, another character exclaimed, "My soul is magnified today because my eyes have seen great things, for salvation is born to Israel!" Exceptional praise is given to God at the arrival of his Messiah.

Although these legends aren't historical, they reflect an acknowledgment of the declarations in Mary's *Magnificat*. They also give us insight into how the earliest Christians understood Mary. In these accounts, as in the Bible, she embraced her role by giving herself as a vessel for God to use for his purpose of redemption. Because of her devotion, God was pleased to use her to bring salvation to the world (Luke 1:54).

APPLICATION

At times we need someone who understands and relates to our situation to come alongside us. Elizabeth served as that person for Mary, and when Elizabeth blessed her, Mary was filled with praise and broke into song. In the words of the *Magnificat*, Mary sang of her devotion to God's will for her life. She sang from her heart, declaring her praise and thankfulness to God for his provision and the immense blessing he had granted in appointing her to give birth to his Son. Her song still resounds with her servant-hearted devotion to God. She then sang from her history, as one of God's people, recounting his intercession and compassion "from generation to generation" (Luke 1:50). When she declared "he has ... exalted those of humble estate," we know she was thinking of Israel as well as herself.

Mary's song reminds us of how God chooses to work through one seemingly insignificant person to advance his work as a whole—for the world, the kingdom, and the believers who will become the Church. Without regard for the shame or danger she might face, Mary devoted herself in service to God, a model of obedience to the generations of believers that continues to this day.

Mary exemplified what the Apostle Paul talks about in 1 Corinthians 12 when he discusses the body of Christ: "For just as the body is one and has many members ... so it is with Christ. ... God arranged the members in the body, each one of them, as he chose" (1 Cor 12:12, 18). Just as God chose Mary to bring his Son into the world, he has a role for each of us to play in his great plan of salvation. Our role may be big or small. It may bring attention to us, or we may go unnoticed. Whatever call God places on our lives, like Mary, we must embrace his plan knowing that we exist to magnify the Lord.

DISCUSSION

A Closer Look

1. Who has God placed in your life to reinforce and confirm his plan and call for you?

_____

_____

_____

2. In what ways do you express praise and thankfulness to God? Do you have a favorite hymn or song that expresses your devotion?

_____

_____

_____

Throughout the Bible

1. Have you ever written songs or poems of praise to God? If you were to do so, what themes or which of God's actions would you focus on?

_____

_____

_____

2. How do our lives identify with God's great redemptive work of the past? How does this help us understand our role in God's ongoing story of redemption?

_____

_____

_____

Beyond the Bible

1. What did Mary give up by embracing her role? Can you think of things that you've given up for the sake of the gospel?

_____

_____

_____

2. What do these birth legends teach us about the early Christian communities? Can you think of Christmas legends that have developed in your understanding of Jesus' birth?

_____

_____

_____

Application

1. Have you discovered what role God is asking you to play in his plan to redeem the world? What can you do to devote yourself to that calling?

_____

_____

_____

2. In the *Magnificat* Mary painted many pictures of God—as conqueror, judge, provider, and helper. Which of these images resonates most with you right now? Why?

_____

_____

_____

CHAPTER 3

A UNIQUE BIRTH

Read Luke 2:1–20.

SETTING THE STAGE

Theme. God seems to delight in defying our expectations. When he reveals part of his plan, we speculate and anticipate until we're pretty certain we've figured out the next phase. Then he steps in and overthrows all our conclusions. The real surprise, though, should be that God includes us in his plans at all. Often, he shocks us most in the people he selects to accomplish his work.

Mary's anticipation of the birth of her son—the promised King—grew with each flutter of movement, evidence of the new life inside her. As her body swelled, she probably imagined what it would be like to give birth to God's Son. Mary's quiet reflection after giving birth to Jesus in a stable suggests that she recognized the incongruity of their circumstances (Luke 2:19). The Messiah had been born as a commoner, not a king. The anticipated ruler had arrived without human fanfare—celebrated by only a few shepherds. When Mary "treasured up all these words," she was not merely cherishing a tender moment with her newborn son. Mary had been given a glimpse into God's plan—one that involved a lowly teenage peasant girl and a group of poor shepherds. Her story reminds us that God can accomplish his plans through anyone and anything. All we can do is prepare to be surprised and resolve to devote ourselves to his plan over our own.

Literary Context. So far, Luke has presented Mary and Elizabeth's stories side by side. Their experiences were parallel: Each woman learned of her pregnancy from Gabriel, each was informed that her son would be great, and each was given instructions for naming her son. But the two women shared no common ground in their birth stories. Elizabeth gave birth to John surrounded by family and neighbors, who celebrated John's arrival with her (see Luke 1:57–58). Mary experienced a less traditional delivery.

Watching her body swell with her first pregnancy, Mary was likely eager to greet her new child, yet also apprehensive at the prospect of giving birth. But her anxiety would have been quieted by the knowledge that she would endure her labor braced by the encouragement of other mothers—women who would then share her joy upon hearing his first infant cries, feeling his miniature fingers and toes, caressing his tender cheek.

This solace dissolved as Mary's due date approached. Caesar's decree denied her the support of family and friends, forcing her and Joseph to instead embark on an 85-mile journey from Nazareth to Bethlehem. The crowds clogging all the available housing eliminated the opportunity for even a traditional delivery; finding nowhere else to spend the night, Mary gave birth in a stable and laid her child in a manger (Luke 2:4–7). Rather than being congratulated by throngs of familiar faces, Mary and Joseph were visited by local shepherds—strangers—who had learned of the newborn Messiah from a startling encounter with the heavenly host (Luke 2:8–17).

Although Elizabeth and Mary did not share a common birth experiences, both women acted in obedience to God's will, as demonstrated by their naming of their sons according to Gabriel's instructions. Mary's delivery, which would have been unusual even for a normal child, was the opposite of what was expected for the birth of the Messiah. Yet her experience was just another example of God defying human expectations. By this point, Mary probably knew that she could no longer predict God's plan for her and her son. As she felt the first pangs of labor while tucked away in a stable, away from her home, family, and support, Mary understood that she would just have to be content with trusting him.

Historical & Cultural Background. Under normal circumstances, there would have been no reason for Mary to give birth in Bethlehem instead of at her home in Nazareth. Yet world events demanding a cross-country trip intervened at a most inconvenient time. Luke records that a decree from Caesar Augustus required all the inhabitants of the Roman Empire to register for the census, undoubtedly to facilitate the collection of taxes.

Following Jewish custom, the people registered according to their ancestral property divisions. For Mary and Joseph, this meant traveling to the territory of the clan of David, which was in the southern region of Judah in the area of Bethlehem—about 80–90 miles from Nazareth, which was located in the northern region of Galilee. Luke skims over the details of the couple's arduous journey, saying only that Joseph "went up" from Galilee to Judaea (Luke 2:4). We can presume that they most likely traveled with a caravan of people making the same trip (see Chapter 2). Mary may have been required to register as well since she was Joseph's wife, or Joseph may have brought her with him simply because he did not want to miss the important event of the birth. Even without the exact details, we can imagine Mary's discomfort and anxiety in traveling during the late stages of her pregnancy.

> **Quick Bit:** At first glance, Luke's description of Augustus' decree as taking place "when Quirinius was governor of Syria" (Luke 2:2) seems problematic since it is not attested to outside of the Bible. The Jewish historian Josephus mentions that a census was carried out by Quirinius in AD 6,[1] but this date does not coincide with Jesus' birth during the days of Herod (whose reign ended in 4 BC).[2] In describing the decree as the "first registration" (Luke 2:2), Luke may have used the Greek word *prōtos*—typically understood as "first"—to mean "earlier" or "before."[3] If so, then Luke refers to a census carried out by Quirinius earlier than the one of AD 6.

As Mary trekked down the long, dusty road to Bethlehem beside Joseph, feeling more discomfort each day from the growing child, thoughts of giving birth to God's Son—the long-awaited Messiah—on the roadside likely plagued her. Although God prevented her fear from becoming a reality, the circumstances under which he brought his Son into the world still fell short of Mary's—and all of Israel's—expectations. Following the glorious manner in which she had learned of her pregnancy, Mary may have held hopes for an equally incredible birth. Knowing that her son would "reign over the house of Jacob forever" (Luke 1:33), she may have expected his delivery to be a time of great celebration or coronation.

When she went into labor in a stable, Mary was probably shocked to realize that she would give birth to this promised King in such lowly and lonely circumstances. Yet this was God's will for the birth of his Son.

A CLOSER LOOK

Contemporary people have to make a huge imaginative leap to put themselves in Mary's place. As the second chapter of Luke opens, nearly six months have passed since Mary left Elizabeth (Luke 1:56), and Jesus' birth is imminent. Today doctors advise pregnant women to avoid any rigorous travel during their third trimester. This is apparently not the case for Mary, as she and Joseph set out on the long journey from Nazareth to Bethlehem to register, despite Mary's rapidly approaching due date.

At first glance Luke's brief treatment of Mary's delivery may seem surprising; he focuses on the response to the birth more than the birth itself. Luke succinctly reports that Mary comes to full term, gives birth, wraps the baby, and lays him in a manger while they are in Bethlehem (Luke 2:6–7). Luke's description lacks the details present in earlier scenes such as the angelic announcements and Mary's visit with Elizabeth. The window into Mary's heart and mind that opened during her encounter with Gabriel has mostly closed, and the reader is left to glean insights into Mary's life and thoughts from a few scattered references to her reactions.

Luke then tells of the angelic announcement of Jesus' birth, which further emphasizes the humble circumstances of the Messiah's birth. Not only is Jesus born in lowly circumstances—his birth is announced to common, ordinary shepherds, and not to the privileged and powerful leaders of the day.

> **Quick Bit:** Although the shepherds were common laborers, the popular depiction of them as the lowest and most despised faction of Jewish society is an exaggeration. In general, the Bible portrays shepherds positively and uses the image as a metaphor for kingship and later church leadership (e.g., Ezek 34:23; Eph 4:11; 1 Pet 2:25). Notable figures such as Abraham, Moses, and David were shepherds. The shepherds' receipt of the message and obedient response helps bring to life the image from the *Magnificat* of God bringing down the

mighty and exalting the humble (Luke 1:52). The Messiah's birth was announced to the poor, not the powerful.[4]

As Mary is enjoying her first tender moments with her son, a troop of local shepherds have already gathered together in the fields for the night, preparing to take turns at the watch, as was customary. They are startled when an angel of the Lord shatters the nighttime stillness with the joyous proclamation that the Messiah has been born (Luke 2:8). The divine light accompanying the angel's sudden appearance would have been blindingly bright even in the daytime; in the darkness of the night, it must have been overwhelming. The angel's appearance on this dark night symbolizes the spiritual reality behind Jesus' birth foreshadowed in Isaiah 9:2: The light of salvation has come into the world.

Thus far in Luke's Gospel, extreme fright has typified the reaction to angelic appearances. Each angelic appearance in Luke has followed the same basic pattern: The angel appears, the people are terrified, and the angel calms their fears and offers a sign to certify that his message is credible. The shepherds' reaction aligns with this pattern. After calming their fears, the angel declares the "good news" that the "Savior," the "Christ," has been born that day in Bethlehem (Luke 2:10–11). In his announcement the angel draws on OT references to the coming day when God will intervene in Israel's history to restore their relationship with him (Isa 40:9; 43:11; 45:1; Dan 9:25). To emphasize the truth of his message, the angel offers the shepherds a sign: The baby will be wrapped in the usual way, "in strips of cloth," but he will be found in an unusual place: "a manger" (Luke 2:12).

> **Quick Bit:** Mary responds to the shepherds' report by treasuring and pondering their words (Luke 2:19). The Greek word for "treasured up," *syntēreō*, can refer to keeping something safe or close by. It indicates careful concern and consideration and resembles other biblical texts where someone ponders significant events, such as Daniel 7:28.[5] Mary is not merely enjoying a happy moment with her new baby—she is carefully contemplating the entire revelation she has received up to this point.

Before the shepherds can mull over the meaning of the sign, they are overwhelmed by the sight of a multitude of angels giving glory to God

(Luke 2:13-14). With the angels' hymn still echoing in their ears, they rush into Bethlehem to see the baby for themselves. We don't know how difficult their search is, as Luke reports in one breath that "they went hurrying and found both Mary and Joseph, and the baby who was lying in the manger" (Luke 2:16).

Seeing the sign given by the angel fulfilled, the shepherds are inspired to recount their entire experience to Mary, Joseph, and apparently anyone else who will listen. Luke says "all who heard were amazed" as the shepherds tell their story (Luke 2:18). While all the other onlookers marvel over the news, however, Mary quietly reflects on all that is happening around her and all that she has been told (Luke 2:19).

As Mary "treasure[s] up all these words, pondering them in her heart," she is likely struck by the simplicity of her surroundings and her unexpected visitors. Or maybe she is wrestling with what God's sending his Messiah into such humble and ordinary circumstances might mean. Although Mary doesn't understand everything perfectly, she realizes something profound and significant has happened. The full cost of her choice to be part of God's plan only becomes clearer with time.

THROUGHOUT THE BIBLE

In the OT, God regularly provided his people with tangible signs and physical symbols as additional means of confirming divine revelation. The angel's statement in Luke 2:12 that "this will be the sign for you" echoes this tradition. For the shepherds the sign of finding the child "lying in a manger" confirmed the truth of the angel's announcement. In seeing it fulfilled, they gained confidence in the rest of the angel's declaration. God's use of prophetic signs has always served to reassure those he called to his purpose, and such signs often made a significant difference when the calling involved something difficult or seemingly illogical.

> **Quick Bit:** The NT use of the Greek word *sēmeion*, or "sign," generally reflects the influence of the OT image of the prophetic sign. The sign is often a miracle or unusual circumstance that points to something the person receiving the sign needs to do or understand. Frequently, the signs accompany the sharing of divine truth

and serve to reinforce that the messenger is really sent by God (Mark 16:20; Acts 5:12; 1 Cor 14:22).

In Judges, Gideon needed reassurance after God called him to deliver Israel from the Midianites (Judg 6:17). God gave him a sign using a wool fleece and the morning dew (Judg 6:36–40). Similarly, after God called Moses to deliver Israel from Egypt, Moses questioned him. God's reply resembles the angel's words in Luke 2:12: "this will be the sign for you" (Exod 3:12). The prophets often used similar language when they preached messages received from God (1 Sam 2:34; 10:7; Isa 7:11; 37:30; 38:7). Sometimes the prophet himself acted out the sign, symbolically reinforcing the divine message (Isa 20:3; Ezek 4:3).

These signs never make much sense on their own, and they're not supposed to. For the shepherds, the newborn lying in a manger would have been unremarkable without the angel's description of what the sign represented. The message and the sign went hand in hand: The message was necessary for understanding the sign, and the sign confirmed the message and proved that the messenger could be trusted. The shepherds responded in praise when they found the baby just as the angel said they would. In doing so, they realized that the angel's message was trustworthy, and they reminded Mary that her son's humble birth was indeed remarkable: This baby was the long-awaited Savior.

BEYOND THE BIBLE

Jesus' advent defied everyone's expectations. His conception by the power of God, the lowly and humble manner of his delivery, the host of angels heralding his arrival to ordinary shepherds—almost everything about Jesus' arrival ran counter to what was expected of the Messiah.

But another surprising aspect of this story is *who* God used to bring the Savior into the world. Mary was young, unmarried, and poor; she wasn't from a wealthy or royal Israelite family—the pedigree that might be expected for the nation's deliverer. And perhaps most surprising: she was a woman. Rarely in antiquity were women offered a prominent place in such significant events. They were more often disparaged, particularly in ancient Jewish culture. With a few notable exceptions, men received the recognition and honor throughout history, especially in ancient Near Eastern and Middle Eastern contexts.

Early Christians viewed Mary as one who reversed these traditions and elevated women to a prominent place in God's work. She did so by obeying God and embracing his role for her. And since her son brought salvation to the world, she played a key role in God's plan for the redemption of humanity. Origen (ca. AD 185–253), a prominent theologian in the early church, emphasized this when he said, "[S]alvation had its first beginnings from women."[6] Centuries later, Bede (ca. AD 672–735)—a learned Christian thinker—elaborated on this point: "Because death made its entrance through a woman, it was fitting that life return through a woman. The one, seduced by the devil through the serpent, brought a man the taste of death. The other, instructed by God through the angel, produced for the world the Author of salvation."[7] Through this contrast with Eve, Bede portrays Mary as the bearer of life who counteracted the effects of the curse (Gen 3:8–24).

That Mary is an exception in the annals of history shouldn't surprise us. A review of God's past redemptive activity makes sense of this role reversal. Throughout the biblical narrative, God delights in using improbable people—a fact highlighted by the less-than-reputable women in Jesus' genealogy (Tamar, Rahab, Ruth, Bathsheba; Matt 1:1–17). He can use anyone and anything to achieve his purposes, including a young, unmarried, peasant girl in first-century Israel.

APPLICATION

Mary's experience of giving birth to her son—God's Son—was different from any birth before or since. As she wrapped his newborn body and held him in her arms, her heart must have swelled with the overwhelming love of a mother for her child. After the angelic announcement, the months of pregnancy, and the trek to Bethlehem, she must have been relieved to rest and do nothing but gaze at the baby in her arms—even if they were in a stable. Like any new mother, she would have held him close, marveled as he wrapped his tiny fingers around hers, and waited expectantly for the next time he opened his eyes to look up at her.

Yet Mary couldn't forget, even for a moment, that her son was unlike any other. He was a king, the long-awaited Messiah. After the shepherds' visit, Luke tells us, "Mary treasured up all these things, pondering them in her heart" (Luke 2:19). She had much to treasure already—including the words of Gabriel, Elizabeth, and the shepherds praising her son. How proud and elated she must have felt to see that her son was already being recognized and set apart. In this, Mary was like all mothers: She took pride in the honor and respect shown to her son.

But as the Greek word for "treasured up" implies, Mary had many other concerns and considerations to ponder. She was taking part in God's grand and glorious plan because she'd agreed to be his humble servant. Still, there was so much she didn't understand. In "pondering" all these things, she likely wondered what being the mother of the Messiah would be like. Thus far, her experience as a mother was far from typical. Even so, Mary's ignorance of what the future held didn't keep her from showing utmost devotion to God and the baby in her arms. In this, Mary is a model for how we should conduct ourselves in the midst of God's work, even when we have little understanding of where it will lead.

DISCUSSION

A Closer Look

1. Have you ever caught yourself pondering in wonder at the ways God has involved you in his plans?

_____

_____

_____

2. Imagine yourself in Mary or Joseph's place in this story: traveling for days, giving birth in a stable, and receiving unexpected visitors. How would you react? What would you ponder?

_____

_____

_____

Throughout the Bible

1. Think of a time when you were perplexed by the way God chose to work. What Scriptures worked like "signs" in your life, reassuring you of God's love and guidance?

_____

_____

_____

2. What ways might God still use today to give us "signs" that confirm his plan and point us in the right direction?

_____

_____

_____

Beyond the Bible

1. Why would God's use of a female surprise a first-century audience? How is Mary's role reversal like Jesus'? How did both defy expectations?

_____

_____

_____

2. Can you think of other women in the Bible who have played major roles in God's story of redemption?

_____

_____

_____

Application

1. Consider how much Mary's life changed in nine short months. What do you think was the hardest challenge for her? How did she handle that challenge?

_____

_____

_____

2. Mary models devotion to God's greater work. Do you recognize your place in his work? How could you be more aware of God's plan and your place in it?

_____

_____

_____

CHAPTER 4

A FORETELLING OF SACRIFICE

Read Luke 2:21–40.

SETTING THE STAGE

Theme. Following God's plan isn't always easy. Even when we're walking in his will, we may still encounter unexpected roadblocks that require us to give more, sacrifice more. But this is what devotion means: accepting the suffering and difficulties along with God's blessing, and remaining committed throughout.

Mary's journey in becoming the mother of Jesus required her to sacrifice her honor in becoming an unwed mother. However, this sacrifice came with the good news that she would give birth to the Messiah, the long-awaited deliverer (Luke 1:32–33). After Jesus' birth, Mary continued to show humble obedience as she and Joseph presented him at the temple. This joyful event, however, was tarnished by the foreboding news of coming discord and the promise of future conflict and emotional pain (see Luke 2:35). Mary learned that in following God, she would confront anguish and sacrifice as God used her son to fulfill his plan of salvation in an unexpected way.

Literary Context. From the moment Gabriel entered Mary's life and delivered the news that she would bear God's son, Mary's milestone experiences—her betrothal, conception, and the birth of her first child—defied tradition. Once she held her newborn son in her arms, Mary was probably eager to experience what remaining Jewish customs she could—including circumcising the baby and presenting him at the temple.

In the Gospel of Luke, Mary followed the prescribed traditions precisely as she and Joseph bundled up the infant Jesus and traveled to the temple to present him to God. Luke's placement of this presentation story indicates Mary and Joseph's reverence toward God and their desire to adhere to biblical law. Luke 2:21, a transitioning verse between these events, shows that Mary and Joseph obeyed not only the biblical law, but also Gabriel's instructions. They followed biblical law by circumcising their son on the eighth day (see Lev 12:3) and carried out Gabriel's naming instructions by calling him Jesus (see Luke 1:31; Matt 1:21).

Mary and Joseph's faithful devotion to the rituals and requirements of first-century Judaism shows that Jesus came from an observant Jewish family—a detail that Luke emphasizes. In a sense, Jesus' family and upbringing served to legitimize his religious significance. Jesus and his family were not rebels or apostates intent on undermining the faith of their people. They showed devotion by participating in the religious heritage of the Jewish nation. But if Mary was hoping for a common experience, she was sorely disappointed. What should have been a joyous occasion instead introduced dread into Mary's dreams for her son's future.

Historical & Cultural Background. When her son was just eight days old, Mary prepared for his circumcision, as countless mothers had before her. Although the practice of circumcision that Mary and Joseph followed is spelled out in Leviticus 12:1–8, God actually established it much earlier. In Genesis 17, God instructed Abraham to circumcise all males in his household (Gen 17:10) as a tangible sign of God's covenant with him (Gen 17:11, 13). God also instructed that every male be circumcised at eight days old (Gen 17:12).

In addition, biblical law ordered that the 33 days following the circumcision be set aside for purification of the mother (see Lev 12:4). At the conclusion of this period, the mother was required to bring a lamb as a burnt offering and a pigeon or turtledove as a sin offering (Lev 12:6–7). If the mother was too poor to provide a lamb, she could offer two pigeons or turtledoves instead (Lev 12:8). The priest took the sacrifice and made atonement for the mother, who was then considered ritually clean or pure (Lev 12:7).

Quick Bit: In biblical usage, the categories of "clean" and "unclean" refer to a state of ritual purity or impurity rather than hygiene. Biblical law contains very detailed instructions for remaining ritually pure and restoring purity after certain defiling events. These instructions were designed to protect the sanctity of any place made holy by God's presence. Requirements for purity or cleanness increased as one drew closer to God's earthly presence. Impure or unclean persons were not allowed to enter the temple or participate in sacrifices.

Mary's obedience to the law and God's call in her life demanded sacrifice—both of time and money, which she and Joseph likely didn't have in abundance. Since Mary brought only a pair of turtledoves or pigeons to Jesus' presentation at the temple (Luke 2:24), we know that she and Joseph were poor. Yet this step in her journey also led her to an unexpected encounter with Simeon, a man whose prophecy brought both blessing and foreboding: He affirmed her son's great role as Messiah, but he also prophesied that before God's plan of salvation would be fulfilled, she would experience anguish due to his mission.

A CLOSER LOOK

Although we desire unique experiences, it can be exciting to take part in traditional milestone events. Imagine Mary's natural desire to participate in familiar cultural rituals. Her role as the mother of Christ has kept her from experiencing many of the cultural norms of her time, and Mary was determined to take part in the traditional purification and dedication rituals that remain. In Luke 2:21–24, Luke interweaves four OT rituals and ceremonies into his narrative: circumcision of the infant, purification of the mother, presentation of the firstborn, and dedication of the firstborn.

In accordance with biblical law, Mary and Joseph circumcise Jesus when he is eight days old. The scene that follows in Luke's Gospel—Mary and Joseph's presentation of Jesus in the temple—occurs about 33 days later (based on the allusion to Lev 12:4–6 in Luke 2:22). Luke's wording in 2:22 suggests that they visit Jerusalem solely to present Jesus at the temple. Yet their visit also signals the end of Mary's period of uncleanness resulting from the birth of Jesus (see "Setting the Stage"). In addition to presenting Jesus at the temple, they travel to Jerusalem to offer the necessary sacrifice for Mary's purification.

> **Quick Bit:** Some of the traditions in the Bible don't make much sense to a modern audience. But the Jews had a purpose for them. If you ever wonder what they're all about, try looking them up in a book like *Nelson's Illustrated Manners and Customs of the Bible*.

Jesus is also Mary's firstborn son, and biblical law stipulated that the firstborn of all creatures was to be devoted to God (Exod 13:2; 34:19–20; Num 18:15–17). Devotion of the firstborn was handled differently for animals and humans. For the firstborn of animals, devoting them to God involved sacrificing them. Firstborn sons, however, were redeemed through the paying of a redemption price, which occurred when the infant was one month old (Num 18:16). Paying this price "redeemed" the firstborn son from the obligation to be devoted to God. Because Jesus is a little over one month old at this time, their trip to the temple combines Mary's purification with the "redemption" of Jesus.

> **Quick Bit:** In ancient Near Eastern culture, the first male offspring of humans and animals was believed to belong to the gods. At times, this belief led to child sacrifice. Rather than sacrifice their firstborn children (which was forbidden by biblical law), the Israelites sacrificed the firstborn of their animals. Regarding their firstborn sons, they either devoted them to divine service or redeemed them by paying the redemption price (Exod 34:19–20; Num 18:15–17).

By combining these events into one, Luke's account blurs some important details. The sacrifice described in Luke 2:24 fits the requirement from biblical law for Mary's purification (Lev 12:1–8), but Luke never mentions the paying of the redemption price. This omission is probably intentional—there is no need to redeem Jesus from divine service because his very presence on earth fulfills God's plan. By virtue of his identity, Jesus is set apart for divine service from his birth.

Luke further emphasizes Jesus' divinely ordained mission by alluding to the OT: "Every male that opens the womb will be called holy to the Lord" (Luke 2:23; see Exod 13:2; 34:19). This reference connects Jesus' birth and childhood with that of the OT prophet Samuel, whose mother, Hannah, specifically dedicated him to the service of God (1 Sam 1:11, 24–28). Despite her barrenness, God blessed Hannah with a son, whom she subsequently "lent to Yahweh" for "as long as he live[d]" in a dedication ceremony (1 Sam 1:27). Luke draws on Hannah's actions in 1 Samuel 1 and casts Jesus' presentation at the temple as a dedication ceremony as well, further highlighting the consecrated nature of Jesus' mission.

Mary is rewarded for following the law's requirements with two unexpected encounters in the temple courts, both of which confirm the special status of her infant son. She first meets an elderly man named Simeon and then an elderly widow named Anna. Luke depicts both individuals as righteous and devout followers of God. God preserves both of them into their old age and enables them to recognize Jesus as the long-awaited Messiah when he arrives in the temple.

Although Luke does not call Simeon an OT prophet, his description of Simeon as a "righteous and devout" man who receives revelation from God through the Holy Spirit certainly fits the image of one (Luke 2:25–26). Simeon has been awaiting the "consolation of Israel"—a phrase that alludes to the ultimate fulfillment of God's promises to restore and save Israel (see Isa 40:1; 49:13). The OT hope for national deliverance eventually coalesces around the figure of a deliverer—the Messiah. Simeon has waited his entire life to see this promise fulfilled. He knows the fulfillment is imminent, as God has revealed it will be in his lifetime (see Luke 2:26). The day finally comes, and the Holy Spirit leads Simeon to the temple as Mary and Joseph arrive with the infant Jesus (Luke 2:27).

Upon seeing Jesus, Simeon responds by praising God (Luke 2:28). He acknowledges that God has fulfilled not only his promise to him personally but has finally brought the promised salvation for his people. Simeon's words of praise reveal to Mary and Joseph that he, too, recognizes the child as the Messiah (Luke 2:29–32). Mary and Joseph are astonished by Simeon's unexpected recognition of what God has also revealed to them (Luke 2:33).

Simeon then blesses Mary, Joseph, and Jesus, but his concluding words foreshadow the challenges that lie ahead. While Simeon rejoices in the arrival of the Messiah, he also warns Mary that many will not accept Jesus as the Messiah. He declares that before coming to unite and restore,

Jesus is appointed to divide the nation and suffer opposition from those he came to save (Luke 2:34). The challenges he will face will one day will cause Mary great emotional suffering—a sword will pierce her soul (Luke 2:35). While Luke fails to describe Mary's reaction to this disturbing news, Mary undoubtedly adds this encounter to the growing catalog of things to ponder as she experiences this unfolding of God's plan (see Luke 2:19).

Mary and Joseph then meet an old widow named Anna who spends her days serving in the temple. This time Luke explicitly identifies her as a "prophetess," making her the female counterpart to Simeon's prophetic witness (Luke 2:36). Anna has lived as a widow for most of her adult life; with the arrival of Mary and Joseph, she is at least in her mid-80s (Luke 2:37). Upon seeing the child, Anna praises God, just as Simeon has. She then begins proclaiming to everyone that the redemption of Israel is at hand (Luke 2:38).

These two unexpected encounters transform Mary and Joseph's trip to fulfill their obligations to the law into a remarkable experience of worship—one that will resonate deeply with Mary and Joseph as they begin their life as new parents. Yet as Mary returns home to Nazareth, the weight of Simeon's prophecy must weigh heavily on her heart as she comprehends the challenges that will come in raising her son. From her obedient devotion to the path that God has laid before her, we learn that we, too, must be willing to turn our backs on the easy and ordinary if we want to live the extraordinary life of walking closely with God.

THROUGHOUT THE BIBLE

Since the Gospels primarily tell us the story of Jesus' adulthood, they include little information about the years between Jesus' dedication and the beginning of his public ministry (with the exception of Luke 2:41–52). Yet this was the time when Mary's role in Jesus' life was most prominent. Luke 2:40 suggests that she must have been doing something right, as it notes that "the child was growing and becoming strong, filled with wisdom, and the favor of God was upon him." This statement, which summarizes a period of 12 years, provides an important clue into Jesus' personal and spiritual development during his younger years. It identifies him as possessing "the favor of God"—a description also used of Mary and a detail crucial for understanding his role.

The concept of obtaining God's favor appears throughout the OT, particularly in the Wisdom books (Job–Song of Solomon). The book of Psalms connects God's favor with the righteous: "For you bless the righteous, O LORD; you cover them with favor as with a shield" (Psa 5:12).[1] Psalm 84:11 presents a similar idea: "For the LORD God is a sun and shield; he bestows favor and honor. No good thing does the LORD withhold from those who walk uprightly." The same connection occurs in the book of Proverbs: "The good obtain favor from the LORD, but those who devise evil he condemns" (Prov 12:2; see also 14:9). The Wisdom books also connect God's favor with wisdom, the dominant theme in Proverbs: "For whoever finds [wisdom] finds life and obtains favor from the LORD" (Prov 8:35).

To hold God's favor, then, is to possess both righteousness and wisdom, which ultimately results in divine blessing. Although God's favor is presented throughout Scripture as something that one should seek and cherish, only three people are described with phrases like, "the favor of God was upon him": Noah, Samuel, and Jesus (Gen 6:8; 1 Sam 2:21, 26; Luke 2:40).

In Noah's day, "The LORD saw that the wickedness of humankind was great in the earth, and that every inclination of the thoughts of their hearts was only evil continually" (Gen 6:5). The text then draws a sharp contrast with Noah: "But Noah found favor in the sight of the LORD" (Gen 6:8). As a result, he and his family were spared when God destroyed the world with the floodwaters (Gen 7:21–23).

Like Noah, Samuel lived during a lawless time. The period of the judges was a period of extreme wickedness—a time when "all the people did what was right in their own eyes" (Judg 17:6; 21:25). Through Samuel, God restored righteousness and justice throughout the land (1 Sam 7:3–4). The text not only says that Samuel "grew up in the presence of the LORD" (1 Sam 2:21), but it also uses a phrase strikingly similar to the one used for Jesus in Luke 2:52: "Now the boy Samuel continued to grow both in stature and in favor with the LORD and with the people" (1 Sam 2:26).

The three times we see the phrase "the favor of God" used in reference to a specific person, it appears during times of great salvation and deliverance. God employs a person with his favor to do a great work for his people. In Noah's story, God saved him and his family from destruction to have people with which to begin humanity anew. With Samuel, God provided Israel with a light during their darkest hour (see 1 Sam 3:3, where Samuel is associated with light). In Jesus, we see God's fullest expression of his favor through which salvation is offered to the world (Luke 2:10).

By Jesus' day nearly 1,000 years had passed since Samuel anointed David as Israel's king. Now the Messiah, David's descendant, possessed and proclaimed God's favor—as did his mother, who is also called "favored one" and described as one who has found favor with God (Luke 1:28, 30). Gabriel's announcement to Mary and his identification of her as "favored one" linked her to her son, Jesus—the bearer and giver of God's favor (compare Luke 1:28, 30; 2:40, 52). But despite God's favor, both Mary and her son would experience grief. Through their grief, however, God would extend his favor to the world.

BEYOND THE BIBLE

From the moment Mary learned of the new life growing in her womb, her life and the life of her son became intertwined. Mary's still blurry vision of her future suddenly focused on her child and the greatness he would become. As she delighted in the excitement of those who recognized her son as Messiah, her images of a bright future for her child would only have intensified. But upon hearing Simeon's words, Mary may have realized that her visions were off.

In Luke 2:34-35 Simeon predicts, "Behold, this child is appointed for the fall and rise of many in Israel, and for a sign that is opposed—and a sword will pierce your own soul also, so that the thoughts of many hearts will be revealed!" With these words Simeon not only alluded to Jesus' crucifixion—a violent death that would have been unexpected for God's Messiah—but he also spoke of the pain Mary would experience as mother of the Savior.

John of Damascus (ca. AD 650-750), a theologian of the early Middle Ages, rightly understood the nature of Simeon's prophecy to Mary, stating:

When she saw [Jesus] put to death as a criminal—the man she
knew to be God when she gave birth to him—her heart was torn
from maternal compassion and she was rent by her thoughts as by
a sword. This is the meaning of "and a sword will pierce through
your own soul."[2]

As she cradled her infant son in her arms, Mary may have had intima-
tions of suffering and grief. Yet this was the reality that came with accepting her role in God's plan. As Jesus would later say of himself, "It is
necessary for the Son of Man to suffer many things and to be rejected by
the elders and chief priests and scribes, and to be killed, and to be raised
on the third day" (Luke 9:22).

But as John of Damascus goes on to note that Mary's future anguish would
only be temporary: "Her grief gave way to the joy of the resurrection, the
resurrection which proclaimed him to be God who had died in the flesh."
As God's plan for salvation came into reality through Jesus' death and resurrection, Mary would recognize her grief and sacrifice as painful yet
necessary part of God's work of redemption.

APPLICATION

Presenting Jesus at the temple was supposed to be a joyous time,
but Mary's interaction with Simeon introduced a sense of foreboding
into her experience. The resounding refrain of the *Magnificat* shifted to
a minor key as Mary began to understand that Jesus would not always be
received with honor and rejoicing. Simeon painted a new picture of Jesus'
future life—a life that would require suffering and sacrifice from them
both. Would she live to see him grown? Would he become a tradesman, a
priest, a ruler? While her journey as God's devoted servant hadn't been
easy, she had great occasion to rejoice, as "The Mighty One [had] done
great things for [her]" (Luke 1:49). Yet when Simeon said, "and a sword
will pierce through your own soul also," (Luke 2:35), she must have sensed
that her devotion to God's plan would bring her pain.

Thus far, Mary had already made extreme sacrifices by assenting to God's
plan. Yet God would ask more of her. Luke doesn't record Mary's reaction to Simeon's words, but we can imagine her response based on what

we know her character. She also understood that God was calling her for the sake of "his servant Israel, in remembrance of his mercy, as he spoke to our fathers, to Abraham and to his offspring forever" (Luke 1:54–55). Her devotion would not waver. As Christ's disciples, we must exhibit this same devotion. Later in Luke's Gospel, Jesus describes what this devotion looks like: "If anyone would come after me, let him deny himself, and take up his cross daily and follow me" (Luke 9:23). Still later, as Jesus hung on the cross and his side was pierced with a sword, Mary may have recalled Simeon's words. But until that time, Mary's faith called her to remain strong and devoted.

DISCUSSION

A Closer Look

1. Today, some Christians consider ritual observances to be legalistic or evidence of a weak faith. Reflecting on Mary and Joseph's experience, how can our actions in obedience to God actually reveal a living and vibrant faith?

_____

_____

_____

2. Reflect on a time when God used an ordinary experience to teach you something extraordinary about himself.

_____

_____

_____

Throughout the Bible

1. What can we learn about God's deliverance from the lives of Noah and Samuel? What points in their lives demonstrate God's providence most clearly?

_____

_____

_____

2. How is God's favor shown to the world today? What's the result?

_____

_____

_____

Beyond the Bible

1. Which sacrifice do you think was hardest for Mary? What would you do in her situation? What can her decisions teach us about God's ability to sustain us?

_____

_____

_____

2. Why do you think Jesus had to be a suffering Savior? What did his death and resurrection accomplish?

_____

_____

_____

Application

1. When you encounter difficulties in life, especially if they arise because of your faith, how do you react?

_____

_____

_____

2. If someone gave you a glimpse of your future, or your children's future, would it help or hinder your faith?

_____

_____

_____

CHAPTER 5

FACING FEAR WITH FAITH

Read Matthew 2:1–23.

SETTING THE STAGE

Theme. God rarely lets us see more than a few steps of our path at a time, but that doesn't keep us from longing to peek ahead. But sometimes when we do catch a glimpse of the future—whether through a weather report, a deadly diagnosis, or (as in Mary's case) a prophecy—the knowledge can be crippling. In times like these, it's easy to wander away on our own or refuse to take another step forward. We forget that God will guide us through any difficulty.

Mary had previously learned that she would suffer great tragedy. Now that threat had come to life: King Herod was desperately seeking the Christ child, placing Mary and her child—Jesus—in danger. It would have been easy for Mary to assume that this was the great tragedy she had been dreading. Yet God knew otherwise; in his providence, Christ's appointed time had not yet come. The prospect of fleeing with a toddler was hardly appealing, but God instructed Mary and Joseph to do just that. In doing so, he preserved them and showed that he had a greater plan. Mary's experience reminds us that we, too, can find comfort in knowing that God's hand is at work in our lives as we follow him.

Literary Context. Thus far in our study of Mary's life, we have focused on Luke's Gospel, largely because Mary figures more prominently in Luke 1–2 than anywhere else in the Gospels. The first two chapters of Luke also include more detail about Jesus' early life than the other Gospels.[1] However, Matthew is the only Gospel to record the story of the magi's visit and Mary and Joseph's escape to Egypt.

Matthew places this story immediately after his account of the birth of Jesus. Despite the traditional depictions of the nativity that place the shepherds and wise men visiting the baby Jesus in the stable, the wise men's visit was likely a separate occasion that took place some months after Jesus' birth. Herod's command to slaughter boys two years old and younger in Bethlehem (Matt 2:16) suggests that Jesus was a toddler at this point. If this was the case, the events of Matthew 2:1–23 fell between the episodes described in Luke 2:22–40 and Luke 2:41–52. Compared to Luke, Matthew includes few details about Jesus birth and early years; his main concern is to show how Christ's coming fulfilled OT prophecies. He also focuses very little on Mary, instead presenting events from Joseph's perspective.

Because of her background role in Matthew's account of the magi's visit and the family's escape to Egypt, it's easy to forget the turmoil these events would have brought into Mary's life. A surprise visit from strange men bearing expensive gifts for her toddler would have been overwhelming in itself. The news that Herod was seeking the Messiah, her son, must have turned her blood cold. As Herod's anxiety about the Messiah's birth developed into the massacre of the infants, Mary likely began to further recognize the unique significance of her child and what that might mean for his future, as well as her own.

Historical & Cultural Background. The origin of the wise men—also called magi or astrologers—is unknown, but it's highly likely that they were Zoroastrians from Mesopotamia. The symbolism associated with them has close affinities with Zoroastrian artifacts and writings. Zoroastrians had a keen interest in astrology because they believed that the arrival of savior-type figures would be accompanied by astronomical anomalies.

> **Quick Bit:** Zoroastrianism was a religion from ancient Iran that thrived during the Persian Empire and spread westward after the conquests of Alexander the Great. Zoroastrian priests were called "magi," and their official duties included astrology. Jewish writings

from the Graeco-Roman period occasionally reflect the influence of Zoroastrian ideas.

The wise men probably noticed that a star had appeared over the Jewish royal city of Jerusalem (where David lived) and journeyed there as a result. Then, after learning that Jewish Scripture foretold that Bethlehem was the city where the king would be born (Mic 5:2), they traveled there. The star pointed to where the king would reign, whereas the prophecy pointed to where he would be born.

As Mary and Joseph were adjusting to the demands of raising a toddler, their already hectic life was interrupted by the arrival of wise men eager to honor their son. The young parents had already received affirmation of their son's status through signs from God and blessings from fellow Jews (see Chapter 4). Now they likely watched with bemusement as their son was revered by foreigners and presented with the gifts of a king.

Yet the joy that Mary felt from this visit was no doubt tempered by the awareness that Herod was seeking to kill her child (Matt 2:13). Even without the angel's command, Mary and Joseph had ample reason to flee from the king. Herod the Great was a ruthless ruler, fanatically paranoid about eliminating potential rivals. His lust for fame and lasting glory drove him to build great structures to boost his ego and establish his legacy.

Herod the Great reigned until 4 BC, so the events of Matthew 2 most likely occurred during the last few years of his reign, which were characterized by excessive political intrigue within his own family resulting in executions and assassinations of potential rivals. The new king, Jesus, had been born into a place that already had a king—and that king would stop at nothing to maintain his authority. Herod understood that if a rightful heir were discovered, he could lose his power; he refused to let that happen. His determination forced Mary to place her full trust in God as she, Joseph, and Jesus fled from Herod's jealous wrath.

A CLOSER LOOK

The narrative that Matthew unfolds in Matthew 2:1–23 overflows with surprising twists and unexpected threats. Imagine the bewildering impact on the new parents. Mary and Joseph don't anticipate the men coming from the east to see their child, and they certainly don't expect the Jewish ruler of their region to attempt to kill him (Matt 2:1–12). Likewise, the wise men from the east don't suspect Herod to react with such paranoia to their announcement of a new king's birth. From his troubled reaction, we can see that Herod is certainly not expecting the news that the Messiah—the rightful king to his usurped throne—will be born in his day. Matthew's narrative doesn't alleviate any of this tension. Immanuel—meaning "God with us"—may be present, but God's presence seems difficult to find.

Matthew sets up a multifaceted political backdrop with the complex wording of Matthew 2:1: "Now after Jesus was born in Bethlehem of Judaea in the days of Herod the king...." Mary and Joseph are caught in the middle of political strife centering on a prophecy about their son (Mic 5:2; compare Matt 1:23). The "days of Herod the king" are a terrible time to be seen as a potential heir to the throne. Herod's grip on power is slipping this late in his reign, and he frequently resorts to extreme measures, using fear and terror to reassert his dominance. Yet the wise men don't know any of this prior to their arrival in Jerusalem.

> **Quick Bit:** Given his reputation for ruthlessness, Herod's concern over this potential "heir" comes as no surprise. But Matthew's note that "all Jerusalem [was troubled] with him" is unexpected (Matt 2:3). Wouldn't Jerusalem rejoice at the news that a rightful king has been born—one that will free them from Herod's tyrannical rule? Matthew's comment is an example of narrative foreshadowing. Jesus' arrival shakes the city to the core and inspires Herod to devise a sinister plot to take his life. Years later, Jesus' entry into Jerusalem will similarly stir up the city and initiate a chain of events that culminates in his crucifixion.[2]

When the wise men arrive, they proceed straight to the royal palace in Jerusalem—a logical location to seek the newborn king of the Jews. They are likely shocked to find the reigning king completely surprised by their news. While the story tells us that Herod "was troubled, and all Jerusalem with him" (Matt 2:3), it appears that Herod plays it cool with these unexpected visitors. He gives the wise men the impression that he, too, is excited by the news and wants to find the child to worship him (Matt 2:8).

When Herod tells the wise men about the prophecy of Micah 5:2, he inadvertently confirms the importance of Jesus' birth (see Matt 2:5–8). When the wise men find the child in Bethlehem, the combined witness of the star and Scripture's prophetic pronouncement reinforces their belief that a royal child has been born. Their reaction to Jesus' birth contrasts sharply with Herod's willful and intentional rejection of Jesus.[3]

> **Quick Bit:** Throughout this story, Matthew refers to Jesus as "the child," using the Greek word *paidion*. If *paidion* had a specific age-related meaning, such as "toddler" or "newborn," it could be used to determine Jesus' age. Unfortunately, the term is generic and can be used for any pre-adolescent child, from a week-old baby (Luke 2:21) to a child old enough to play in the marketplace with his friends (Matt 11:16).

After the wise men leave Herod's palace, the star reappears to guide them to the house where Jesus, Mary, and Joseph are residing (Matt 2:9). Upon finding the child, the wise men worship him and give him magnificent gifts fit for a king: gold, frankincense, and myrrh (Matt 2:10–11). Ironically, even as these foreigners journey many miles to pay their respects and shower him with gifts, the Jewish royalty of the day ignore the Messiah. Mary is probably caring for the baby, anticipating taking him home to Nazareth, when she hears an unexpected knock at the door. Despite the reactions Mary has already seen Jesus produce, the sight of a group of foreign travelers who have journeyed miles to see her son must be overwhelming. The unexpected nature of this event further reinforces her faith that God really has chosen her to be the mother of his Son, the Messiah.

Joseph flees with Mary and Jesus to Egypt, leaving under the cover of night. A short time later, Herod realizes that the wise men aren't coming back. Having no other way of identifying the child born "king of the Jews" (Matt 2:2), he orders that all boys in the region of Bethlehem around the age of two and younger be killed (Matt 2:16). Herod questioned the wise men on the timing of the star's appearance; based on their answer, he now determines how old the boy might be. He probably adds some months to the calculation just to be sure. Matthew describes the aftermath of the slaughter by quoting Jeremiah 31:15 about "Rachel weeping for her children" (Matt 2:18). Although no other sources report this event from

Herod's reign, the massacre fits his ruthless, paranoid behavior—especially during the later years of his reign, when his last-ditch attempts to hold on to power increasingly alienate his Jewish subjects.

After Herod dies in 4 BC, Joseph is again notified in a dream that it is safe to return home (Matt 2:19–20). He takes Mary and Jesus and settles in Nazareth (Matt 2:23). Matthew doesn't specify how long they spent in Egypt; his account moves from their flight to Egypt to their return in the span of a few verses, offering no clues as to how much time has elapsed. They may have stayed in Egypt a few weeks, a few months, or perhaps a year. However long their exile, Matthew's account shows us that the young family remains confident in God's provision for them every step of the way.

THROUGHOUT THE BIBLE

The NT writers were steeped in the story, imagery, and theology of the OT. In communicating the gospel message, the NT writers quoted passages or alluded to stories or prophecies that demonstrated how events of their time were grounded in the ongoing plan of God and fulfilled in Christ.

One way the writers accomplished this was to use symbolic parallels—people, places, and events that underscored important truths. Egypt repeatedly played this role because of its relationship to the exodus. Egypt symbolized a place of bondage for Israel (Exod 1–14) as well as a place of refuge (Gen 12:10–20; 46:5–8; Jer 42–43). In bringing his people "out of Egypt," God established his power to save and his willingness to act in history on behalf of his people (Hos 11:1).

Matthew's story of the flight to Egypt finds an unexpected but profound parallel in 1 Kings 11. The OT story describes how King Solomon lost God's favor and how his God-appointed replacement, Jeroboam, had to flee to Egypt to escape the king's wrath. Solomon married many foreign women who led him to worship their foreign gods instead of the true God of Israel. The prophet Ahijah informed Jeroboam, an official of Solomon, that God planned to take the 10 northern tribes away from the dynasty of David and make him king of Israel instead (1 Kgs 11:31). When Solomon learned of this encounter, he tried to kill Jeroboam. Jeroboam escaped by fleeing to Egypt, where he stayed until Solomon died (1 Kgs 11:40).

The symbolic use of Egypt in Matthew's story closely aligns with the account from 1 Kings 11. Just as Jeroboam fled to Egypt to escape the fury of a king, Jesus and his family fled to Egypt to escape the wrath of Herod the Great. Jeroboam had been promised a kingship that he had not yet received. Jesus' parents likewise knew that their son had been promised kingship, but it had not yet been given to him by God. Matthew's use of this parallel casts Mary and Joseph as having symbolically experienced the bondage and redemption of Israel in the exodus.

Another way NT writers used OT texts was through identifying the fulfillment of OT prophecy. Matthew filled his narrative with scriptural allusions and quotations to emphasize the many subtle ways in which OT prophecy anticipated even the details of Jesus' coming. The prophet Micah said the Messiah would come from Bethlehem (Mic 5:2; Matt 2:6). Mary and Joseph's flight to Egypt (Matt 2:13–15) links to Hosea 11:1—a prophecy drawing on the imagery of the exodus. Even the horrible massacre in the area of Bethlehem is connected to the weeping and lamentation predicted by Jeremiah (Jer 31:15; Matt 2:18). At every opportunity, Matthew linked Jesus' story to Israel's Scriptures.

The imagery of Matthew 2 also provides an example of the subtle way in which the OT narrative played out in the details of related NT events. In Numbers 22–24, the prophet Balaam was hired to curse Israel but found God would not let him speak anything but blessings over his people. One of Balaam's blessings pointed to a far-future messianic king who would rule over God's people: "I see him, but not now; I behold him, but not near; a star will go out from Jacob, and a scepter will rise from Israel" (Num 24:17). The image of a star pointing the way to Jesus, the promised Messiah, provided a literal clue to the symbolic fulfillment of Jesus as the "star" and "scepter" that would rule over Israel.

But in Matthew these events are more than just symbols; they marked a new reality. The signs accompanying Jesus' birth and early life surely helped Mary and Joseph understand their place within God's work and gave them hope in the midst of their struggles. Even if Mary and Joseph weren't aware of the symbolism, Matthew's use of these symbols gave his audience a glimpse into how God's work played out in history. We don't always see behind the curtain, but when we do, it's incredible. Hope can be found in apparently desperate, unexpected, and even impossible situations.

BEYOND THE BIBLE

The Messiah was destined to die, but his time had not yet come. News of his birth worried King Herod, who thought that the Messiah would seize his kingdom. Herod's paranoia about retaining his throne compelled him to eliminate all potential rivals—even babies. But not even his dastardly attack on Bethlehem's children could interrupt God's timetable. Instead, God preserved Jesus and his family and showed that he had a greater plan.

An angel instructed Joseph to get his family out of harm's way and flee to Egypt (Matt 2:13). The Bible doesn't tell us anything about their time in Egypt, but countless legends developed over the centuries. The early church was particularly interested in Jesus' interaction with Egypt's pagan culture, and his return to Israel brought to mind God's mighty deliverance through Moses (Exod 12:29–36). Jesus' legendary activities in Egypt gave Christians hope by showing God's preservation of his people in the midst of opposition.

> **Quick Bit:** The *Gospel of Pseudo-Matthew* was probably written around the sixth century AD. It uses the Gospels of Matthew and Luke as an outline but adds many legendary expansions. It also draws on other ancient apocryphal sources. Even though its stories aren't factual, it provides a helpful look into the ways in which early Christian communities understood Jesus as the God-man—fully God and truly human.

Although they're not true stories, these legends show how some early Christian communities understood God's sovereignty—how he brought his Messiah into the world and orchestrated the story of redemption. They claim that God not only protected the holy family during their flight from Herod, but that he also used them to bring about salvation.

The *Gospel of Pseudo-Matthew* recounts some of these experiences. One of its most fascinating stories shows God's preservation of the family en route to Egypt. On the third day of their journey, Mary rested in the shade of a palm tree and expressed her desire to eat the tree's fruit. Joseph lamented that the fruit was out of reach, stating that he would prefer to have water instead. When the infant Jesus heard this, he commanded the palm tree to bow down so they could eat its fruit. *Pseudo-Matthew* describes the scene as follows:

> Then the child Jesus ... said to the palm, "O tree, bend thy branches, and refresh my mother with thy fruit." And immediately at these words the palm bent its top down to the very feet of the blessed Mary; and they gathered from it fruit, with which they were all refreshed. And after they had gathered all its fruit, it remained bent down, waiting the order to rise from him who had commanded it to stoop.[4]

After they ate and were satisfied, Jesus gave the tree another command:

> "[O]pen from thy roots a vein of water which has been hid in the earth, and let the waters flow, so that we may be satisfied from thee." And it rose up immediately, and at its root there began to come forth a spring of water exceedingly clear and cool and sparkling.[5]

God, through Jesus, provided satisfaction for the family's hunger and thirst in the middle of the desert, just as he had for the Israelites when they left Egypt (Exod 15:22; 16:13–15).

An apocryphal story from *The First Gospel of the Infancy of Jesus Christ* depicts another aspect of God's sovereignty. It describes his mighty power through the infant Jesus and was understood as a fulfillment of Matthew 2:15: "Out of Egypt I called my son." On their way to Egypt, the holy family stayed in an inn next to a pagan temple. The temple priest had a young boy who was demon possessed. One day the demon caused the boy to wander into the inn where Jesus and his family were staying. Upon seeing Mary washing Jesus' diapers and hanging them up to dry, the boy walked over, grabbed a diaper, and placed it on his head. As soon as he did this, "the devils began to come out of his mouth, and fly away in the shape of crows and serpents."[6]

Quick Bit: *The First Gospel of the Infancy of Jesus Christ* is also referred to as *The Arabic Gospel of the Infancy*, named after one of its earliest Arabic manuscripts. It's uncertain when this collection of legends was compiled; suggestions range from the second century AD onward. For the early church, its myths about Mary and Jesus functioned to "fill in the gaps" from the biblical Gospels. They were eventually rejected as untrue, but they still provide a helpful look into the ways in which early Christians thought about Jesus.

This entertaining story goes on to praise God for his mighty deliverance. When the boy's father questioned him as to how he became well, the boy credited the power of God. The father responded, "My son, perhaps this boy is the son of the living God, who made the heavens and the earth."[7] Other apocryphal sources say that the priest and the entire population of his city became followers of God. After this incident, Jesus and his family returned to the land of Israel.

These nonbiblical legends show that early Christians believed in God's supernatural protection of his Son. They also believed that he was orchestrating his plan, which nothing could derail. Despite Herod's attempts to eliminate the Messiah, God would not allow Jesus to die before his appointed time. The stories in the apocryphal gospels describe God's providence, sustenance, and might. The early Christians left us a legacy to emulate: They understood God's sovereignty, which gave them the confidence to devotedly follow him.

APPLICATION

At times it can seem as if all the challenges of life bear down on us at once. Despite our faith, we may feel wracked by fear and doubt. Even when we are following in God's will, we can still get caught up in tensions and turmoil. Mary found herself in such a dilemma when Joseph informed her that they must leave for Egypt immediately to protect Jesus from Herod's wrath.

In spite of her unwavering devotion to God, Mary must have felt confused, even torn. She had already learned to trust in God's direction—people with ever-increasing spheres of influence had confirmed Gabriel's message that her son would be the Messiah, including relatives, prophets, and now scholars (the wise men). Although she must have felt joy that so many people were honoring her son—some of them like the wise men traveling long distances to do so—she must have realized that reports of his birth were spreading. Her motherly pride and happiness probably began to yield to fear as Simeon's words—"this child is appointed for the fall and rising of many in Israel, for a sign that is opposed"—rang in her ears (Luke 2:34).

Mary must have been terrified when Joseph learned that King Herod wanted her son dead, and that he would resort to horrifying measures to eliminate any threat to his throne. In addition to fear, she would have been sickened to think of so many young boys being killed, their mothers "[refusing] to be comforted, because they [were] no more" (Matt 2:18). Why was this happening? Jesus was still just a boy. How could her son be king if another king determined to kill him?

Mary must have wondered whether the tragic end prophesied for Jesus was about to take place. She didn't know that this was not Jesus' appointed time to die. She only knew that God had provided for them thus far, and in spite of the fears that assailed her now, she continued to place her trust in God. She prepared her heart and mind for another journey as she and Joseph took Jesus and fled to Egypt.

When we encounter confusion and danger in our lives, we can look to Mary's example of courage and faith. No matter the chaos surrounding her, she surrendered her life—and the life of her son—to God's will. As Proverbs 16:9 tells us, "A man's heart plans his way, but the Lord directs his steps." Even when our path crumbles before us, if we are devoted to God, we can take that next step in confidence and faith.

DISCUSSION

A Closer Look

1. We sometimes think that when we're doing things God's way, it should get easier. How can the events of Matthew 2 help us see God's plan even as we experience trials and persecution?

_____

_____

_____

2. God uses the wise men as an example, showing how people we might not expect can still come to worship God. What can we do to reach out to people in our lives whom we might not expect to respond positively to the message of the Gospel?

_____

_____

_____

Throughout the Bible

1. As readers of the Bible, we get a more complete story of God's plan than the people who lived out these events. How does that point of view enrich or hinder your experience of God through his Word?

_____

_____

_____

2. Read some of the references to Egypt in the second paragraph of this section. Reflect on the different ways that Egypt is used symbolically, both positively and negatively.

_____

_____

Beyond the Bible

1. How does an understanding of God's sovereignty over time and history give you hope for your current situation and your future?

_____

_____

_____

2. Traveling to Egypt through the desert with a baby was almost as dangerous as staying in Bethlehem. Yet God sustained Mary and Jesus. Can you recall a time of God's great sustenance in your life?

_____

_____

_____

Application

1. How would you respond if your child were being threatened? Would you feel angry with God? How would you bring yourself to trust him?

_____

_____

_____

2. God rarely lets us glimpse more than a few steps of our path—our life—at any given time. Do you think this is merciful? Would you rather know exactly how your life will play out? Reflect on why or why not.

_____

_____

_____

CHAPTER 6

PREPARING TO LET GO

Read Luke 2:41–52.

SETTING THE STAGE

Theme. If you're a parent, you might reluctantly admit to having driven off without your child. In the scramble to get on the road, perhaps you forgot to count heads. But imagine returning in a panic only to find that your youngster had *intentionally* stayed behind—and showed absolutely no remorse for giving you the scare of a lifetime. How would you react?

Mary lived through such an experience. She discovered that Jesus was not with them when they left the Passover festival in Jerusalem, and she and Joseph launched a full-scale search. When they finally found him in the temple, he seemed baffled by their frantic worry: "Did you not know that I must be in my Father's house?" (Luke 2:44 ESV). As the mother of God's Son, Mary faced many unusual parenting situations. She knew that God had a plan for Jesus. And although she did not fully understand the details of that plan, this incident at the temple implies that Jesus did. The time had come for Mary to begin relinquishing her control as Jesus' mother, but giving up control was not easy. True devotion often requires that we surrender ourselves to God's plan, even when we don't understand it. For Mary, devotion meant surrendering her maternal instincts to protect and shield her son from danger so he could pursue God's will— the mission for which he was born.

Literary Context. Most of the stories about Jesus recorded in the Bible focus on his ministry as an adult. Only two Gospels (Matthew and Luke) include the account of his birth. Most of Jesus' childhood is summarized in two verses (Luke 2:40, 52) that bookend the account of Mary and Joseph leaving Jesus at the temple (Luke 2:41-51).

Luke concludes his "infancy narrative" (Luke 1:5-2:52) with this story, which also transitions his Gospel from the details of Jesus' birth and dependency on his earthly parents to the story of his ministry and relationship with his heavenly Father. The incident at the temple shows that, even as a child, Jesus was aware of his purpose. Luke's description also shows how his parents struggled to understand God's plan for their son.

Although Mary and Joseph may have brought Jesus to the temple on several occasions, this is only Luke's second story of such a visit (see Luke 2:22-40). In both accounts Mary learns a little more about God's plan for Jesus. In Luke 2:33 she and Joseph marvel at Simeon's prophecy about him. In Luke 2:49 they fail to understand Jesus' response that he must be in the house of his Father. Through these situations we catch a glimpse of the difficulties Mary faced as she devoted her life to raising the Son of God.

Historical & Cultural Background. Just as they did at Jesus' dedication (see Luke 2:22-24), Mary and Joseph acted in faith and obedience to God's commands as they traveled to the temple during Passover. The Law stipulated that the people travel to Jerusalem for three festivals each year: Passover, the Feast of Weeks, and the Feast of Booths (see Exod 23:14-17; Deut 16:16). All males were to appear before God at the temple during each of these feasts. In the first century, Jews who were unable to attend all three feasts would at least attend Passover.[1]

Passover—also known as the Feast of Unleavened Bread[2]—commemorated God's leading his people out of slavery in Egypt (see Exod 12:14-20). Worshipers sacrificed a lamb at the temple (see Exod 12:3-6) and ate the Passover meal in a home or room (see Matt 26:17-19). Jerusalem's population surged with the throngs of devout Jews making their pilgrimage to the temple during this festival. The Jewish historian Josephus once estimated that three million people had come to Jerusalem during Passover.[3]

A parent might easily lose track of a child in such large crowds, as Mary and Joseph did.

As Mary obediently followed God's call on her life, she discovered step by step that she had to give up her son to God's purposes. During an earlier temple visit, Mary had been warned that she would experience suffering (Luke 2:35). Returning to the same place 12 years later, she experienced the first tugs of Jesus breaking away from her and Joseph—his earthly parents—when he explained his heavenly purpose (Luke 2:49). Jesus remained submissive to his parents for a while (Luke 2:51), but the day was approaching when Mary would have to completely surrender him to God's purpose—ultimately standing by to witness as he sacrificed himself on the cross for her redemption and ours.

A CLOSER LOOK

Luke's narrative of Jesus' childhood pitches us forward in time and presents us with a 12-year-old Jesus visiting Jerusalem with his parents—perhaps for the first time since he was an infant. On this occasion we see Jesus between childhood and adulthood. In Jesus' day, a Jewish boy had the full religious responsibilities of an adult at age 13.[4] The years leading up to that coming of age were filled with training to prepare the boy to assume his place in Jewish society. Jesus' trip to Jerusalem may have been part of this preparation. Women and children were not required to attend the festivals in Jerusalem, so Mary and Jesus' participation indicates exceptional devotion. Luke records that Mary and Joseph went to Jerusalem "every year" for the Passover (Luke 2:41), further establishing their character as devoted followers of Jewish traditions. Now Mary and Joseph travel to Jerusalem for Passover just as they have every year, but this time Jesus accompanies them (Luke 2:42).

> **Quick Bit:** Although Luke tells us that Mary and Joseph traveled to Jerusalem for Passover every year, he doesn't specify whether Jesus came along in years past. Luke's silence could indicate that readers should assume Jesus was present every year along with his parents.[5] However, the alternative—that this was Jesus' first visit—makes just as much sense of the available information and fits the tradition of a 12-year-old boy's training before his coming of age at 13.

The journey to Jerusalem for Passover is only the backdrop for this narrative because the event of note takes place *after* the weeklong celebration. Mary and Joseph pack up and set off on the road home, probably traveling as part of a caravan with others from the Galilee region, including friends and relatives (Luke 2:43-4). Mary may be traveling separately from Joseph in the caravan, each one thinking that Jesus is with the other or with relatives in the same caravan. When the traveling party stops for the night, Mary and Joseph realize he is missing. After anxiously checking with all their friends and relatives, they return to Jerusalem to continue their frantic search (Luke 2:45).

If you're a parent, you can easily empathize with Mary and Joseph and the rush of adrenaline and their gasps of horror as they realize their child is missing. Their calls—"Jesus! Jesus, where are you?"—become more frantic as they search the entire caravan for him. Their anxiety grows to fear as the minutes turn into hours and then days—all the while searching for their lost child, wondering if they will ever see him again. For Mary, the anxiety must have been particularly acute: She is the divinely appointed caretaker for the Son of God, and she has lost him. For three days Mary and Joseph search the streets of Jerusalem. On the third day they finally find Jesus in the temple (Luke 2:46)—perhaps he never left.

Overwhelmed by relief after days of anxious searching, Mary finds Jesus sitting in the temple—safe all this time. She sees him listening to the teachers, asking questions, and holding his ground as he discusses religious issues with the leaders of the day. The sight of a 12-year-old boy boldly proclaiming the Scriptures amazes the crowds and surprises his mother. But Mary's relief fades to exasperation as she asks Jesus why he has put them through such a harrowing ordeal (Luke 2:48). His reply discloses a truth that will affect Mary for the rest of her life.

Jesus responds by declaring the primacy of his relationship with God: "Did you not know that it was necessary for me to be in the house of my Father?" (Luke 2:49). The Father-Son relationship trumps every other in his life. His surprise—"Did you not know?"—reveals that he thinks these circumstances should be apparent to Mary. She knows the time is coming when she will have to let him go, but she did not expect it to come so soon. His response shocks Mary into painful awareness: Jesus shows no sense of wrongdoing for staying behind on his own. In fact, he is perplexed by her worry, assuming she would have known exactly what he was doing and where. Their relationship reaches a turning point at this moment. The bond between devoted mother and divine Son is fundamentally and forever changed.

Luke reports that Mary and Joseph "did not understand" Jesus' answer (Luke 2:50), but despite everyone's confusion, Jesus does return with them to Nazareth. Safe at home again, Mary continues to ponder the meaning of Jesus' words and actions (Luke 2:51). The painful, nerve-wracking experience of this temporary loss likely prompts her to recall Simeon's warning (Luke 2:35).[6] Perhaps she begins to understand more of the nature of Jesus' calling—and starts preparing her heart for that future loss when his Father's mission will take precedence over his mother's love.

THROUGHOUT THE BIBLE

In Scripture the defining moment in a prophet's life came when he heard and responded to the call to serve as God's messenger. Although Jesus was much more than a prophet, many viewed him in terms of that role. The people closest to a prophet—family, friends, neighbors, and onlookers—experienced their own moments of discovery, realizing that they were in the presence of someone specially gifted by God. For Jesus and his family, the encounter in the temple was one such moment (Luke 2:45, 29).

Through that event people began to learn about Jesus and his unique gifts, just as others had learned about the prophets before him. Jesus, too, seems to have learned something about himself—or at least he first articulated his awareness of a divine calling. Jesus' response to his parents suggests that this was a learning moment for everyone. He was beginning to recognize that he saw the world and the Scriptures differently—more clearly—than everyone else, and his parents started to comprehend what this meant for their lives (Luke 2:48–49).

The OT prophets were accustomed to being marginalized, rejected, and ostracized (e.g., Isa 7–8; Jer 26–28; Amos 7; 1 Kgs 17). In part their persecution resulted from their ability to see what others didn't (or couldn't), both in the future and the present. They understood God's teachings and either proclaimed truth or refuted error (e.g., Exod 5; 1 Kgs 18; 2 Kgs 7; 19).

They envisioned both heavy judgment and a hopeful future. Their prophecies astonished, frustrated, and confused people. Jesus encountered all of these responses in Luke 2: The people in the temple were astonished, and Mary and Joseph felt both frustrated and confused (Luke 2:46, 48, 50). In the biblical text, this marks the first time that Jesus began to distance himself from Mary. Her path was bound to his, but Jesus' path was his own (see John 19:25–27).

Many biblical prophets seemed independent and detached from normal family relationships (compare 1 Kgs 19:19–21), possibly because their families didn't fully understand them or because their calling required them to be autonomous. At the temple Mary learned through a dramatic and frightening experience what was to become a central theme of Jesus' ministry: Jesus' ways are not our ways for he is perfectly good and holy, and following him requires total surrender (compare Mark 3:33). The young Jesus taught his parents that his mission was just getting started, and they had to understand that his ultimate loyalty was to his Father in heaven. Likewise, we, too, should be prepared to acknowledge and embrace God as our true Father—the Creator of all.

Like Jesus and the prophets before him, Mary was called to live a radical truth. Although her experiences as a young mother were singularly challenging, these moments marked the beginning of the changing world. Not only must Mary follow God with complete devotion, she must also be continually prepared to accept change and increasing sacrifice.

BEYOND THE BIBLE

Ever since Gabriel's proclamation (Luke 1:26–38), Mary's life had been dedicated to accomplishing God's mission: giving birth to and mothering the Messiah. She didn't know God's entire plan, but she knew it wouldn't be an easy path. By surrendering herself to a life of total devotion, she embraced difficulties and a growing awareness that grief and heartache awaited (Luke 2:34–35). Part of her mission was to relinquish her son to God's purposes. As Jesus grew into the mission God had prepared for him, he would rely more on his heavenly Father and less on his earthly mother.

Jesus' life was also dedicated to accomplishing God's mission. He no doubt heard about this mission from his mother (Luke 1:31–33, 35) and grew into greater awareness of it with age. Legends developed around these formative years that demonstrate Jesus' awareness of and devotion to God's plan. These legends exhibit his sense of calling, even as a boy, and show his total commitment to fulfilling his mission. They also foreshadow his ministry and confirm his identity as the Messiah.

Two legends from Jesus' childhood—both allegedly taking place before his sixth birthday—demonstrate this awareness and devotion. While Jesus was playing with his friends on the roof of a house, a boy fell and died. The other children ran away, but Jesus remained. When the boy's parents heard, they rushed to the scene. They saw Jesus alone on the roof and accused him of killing their son. Jesus denied doing so, but they didn't believe him. So to prove his innocence, Jesus asked the dead boy what happened:

> Then Jesus jumped from the roof and stood by the body of the child and cried with a loud voice and said, "Zeno (for that was his name), arise and tell me, did I throw you down?" And immediately he got up and said, "No, Lord, you didn't throw me down, but you did raise me up."[7]

The people's response to Jesus' miracle mirrors those found in the biblical Gospels by people who observed his ministry and miracles: "And when they saw it they were amazed. And the parents of the child glorified God for the sign which had come to pass, and worshiped Jesus."[8]

Quick Bit: Both of these myths come from the *Infancy Gospel of Thomas*, a collection of stories about Jesus' childhood allegedly compiled by the Apostle Thomas (Mark 3:18). This apocryphal or legendary gospel should not be confused with the *Gospel of Thomas*, which is often classified as a "gnostic" writing (from the Greek word for "knowledge"). The *Infancy Gospel of Thomas* is a collection of fictional expansions about Jesus' childhood based on the limited data of the biblical Gospels. These stories grew out of the traditions of some early Christian communities and were used to explain Jesus' childhood in light of his divine and human natures.

A second legend reflects his healing ministry. A young man in Jesus' neighborhood was splitting wood when he lost control of his axe. The wound to his foot left him near death from blood loss. The community gathered to help him, but the situation was hopeless. When Jesus heard, "he also ran to the scene, and forced his way through the crowd. He took hold of the young man's injured foot, and immediately it was healed."[9] The crowd again testified to the work of God in the young Jesus: "But when the multitude saw what was done, they worshipped the young child, saying, 'Truly the spirit of God dwells in this young child.' "[10]

These nonbiblical legends communicate the same awareness that Jesus displays in Luke 2:41-52. Even from a young age, he had a sense of the mission that he was sent to earth to accomplish: His mission would be a life-giving, healing ministry of salvation to the world. And as he grew into his divine mission, he gradually and naturally began to separate from his earthly ties, including his relationship with Mary and the rest of his family. For Jesus to fulfill his role in God's plan, Mary would have to surrender her role as his mother.

APPLICATION

Parents may struggle to step back and let their children become the people God meant them to be. At the same time, children may struggle to honor their parents while asserting their individuality. This is especially true for the firstborns, who must blaze the trail for younger siblings as they and their parents learn to take on new roles. It can be a time of great emotional turmoil for all involved.

Mary knew that the day would come when she would have to step back and let Jesus fulfill the mission for which he had been born. As Jesus approached his 13th birthday—when he would be considered a man under Jewish law—Mary would have been preparing for him to grow into adulthood. But in this transition, Mary had to further surrender her human instincts to an eternal purpose. In her devotion to God's will, she had to let Jesus go to a future she knew would be filled with pain and conflict. That pain erupted in her heart when she and Joseph found Jesus in the temple, and he was stunned by their worry (Luke 2:49). In that moment

Mary was confronted with the full truth: Her son was God's Son. And once again, God called her to surrender to his greater plan.

Total devotion to something greater than ourselves means we must make individual sacrifices. We must surrender our will to the greater plan—even when we lack a full understanding of that plan. In the process of surrender, such devotion transforms into discipleship. Throughout the NT, when Jesus called people to become his disciples, he required that they make a break with their past and leave the trappings of their former lives behind. When Jesus called the rich young ruler to follow him, the man was asked to abandon his possessions (Mark 10:21). Jesus' disciples left everything behind when they responded to his call: their livelihoods (Mark 2:14), their families (Matt 4:20–21), their past (Luke 9:2–6). Recognizing Jesus as Messiah constitutes a turning point—for Mary and for everyone who would obey God.

What a crossroad Mary faced as Jesus rejoined them and returned home! While she had been privy to the early stages of God's plan, she had yet to understand that she must sacrifice her role as Jesus' mother to become his disciple. Mary is the only person who ever faced the transition from mother of God to child of God. Understandably, it would take time for her to accept this change.

DISCUSSION

A Closer Look

1. Reflect on your own experience as a 12- or 13-year-old. How would your parents have reacted if you'd wandered off for three days?

_____

_____

_____

2. Have you ever experienced a time when you had to let go of something you cherished? It could be a friend, a child, a spouse, even an idea. Use that experience to reflect on Mary's growing understanding of letting go of Jesus as he grows up.

_____

_____

_____

Throughout the Bible

1. When did you first realize that Jesus is someone special whom you can trust and believe in?

_____

_____

_____

2. Many biblical prophets and Jesus' own disciples had to leave behind their families and friends for the higher calling of following God. How much would you sacrifice to follow God's call?

_____

_____

_____

Beyond the Bible

1. Do you have a sense of God's mission in your life? What is it, and what part does the gospel play?

_____

_____

_____

2. Has your sense of God's mission caused you to give up certain things in your life? How does your sense of God's mission help you prioritize?

_____

_____

_____

Application

1. If you are a parent, what has been most difficult in letting your children grow up? What were your biggest struggles? What has brought you the most joy?

_____

_____

_____

2. What has Jesus called you to sacrifice in order to follow him?

_____

_____

_____

CHAPTER 7

FAMILY REDEFINED

Read John 2:1–12 and Mark 3:20–35.

SETTING THE STAGE

Theme. When we're wrestling with a difficult transition, we bristle at people who offer a sympathetic, "Change is for the better!" Loath as we are to admit it, however, there's truth in this cliché—it's just difficult to recognize the good in circumstances we don't fully understand. This is especially true when the change forces us to give up something we care about, like a relationship, ministry, or job. In these times, we may look to God in hurt bewilderment. Could this truly be his will? But our sacrifices are never in vain. God's purpose always prevails.

At every unexpected turn of events in her life as Jesus' mother, Mary responded with faith. As she watched her son grow in years and wisdom, she realized ever more acutely that he was his Father's Son, not just her own. Two events early in Jesus' public ministry serve as vivid reminders of this. In each case, when Jesus made statements showing that his attention had shifted to higher priorities—even at the sacrifice of familial relationships—Mary had to face the reality that God's purpose for Jesus was more important than their mother-son relationship. Unlike any other person in history, Mary had to relinquish her son to follow him.

Literary Context. When Jesus returned home from his early evangelization efforts (Mark 3:7–12), he encountered harsh opposition from his family and those in his hometown. Jesus responded by redefining the identity of his family: His true family members were like-minded people who obeyed their heavenly Father (Mark 3:35). This statement distanced Jesus from his biological family and showed that he had a new focus: making disciples. It also demonstrated a shift in his priorities, as his Father's plan took precedence.

We catch glimpses of this priority shift in an earlier event as well. At the beginning of his public ministry, Jesus attended a wedding at Cana with his family and disciples (John 2:1–11). During the festivities, a crisis occurred: The host ran out of wine. Given the serious nature of this social blunder, Mary asked Jesus if he would help. His response reveals that his purposes were governed by something beyond Mary's concerns: "Woman, what does this have to do with me? My hour has not yet come." As Gerald Borchert writes, "Jesus was not being directed by his mother but by a determined hour."[1] Recognizing the shift in Jesus' focus, Mary stepped back and anticipated seeing him in action, instructing the servants, "Whatever he says to you, do it" (John 2:5).

Historical & Cultural Background. Mary's grave concern about the lack of wine may seem out of proportion to us. But in the first century, her distress was justified. Weddings at that time were an important cultural celebration. The celebration itself was a significant event for the bride and groom and their families. The entire community would be involved in the festivities, which typically lasted a week, often with new guests arriving each day.

Guests brought presents and, in return, expected the groom's family to provide a sufficient supply of food and wine. Running out of wine was a major embarrassment for the hosts. In fact, a failure in this important aspect of the celebration left the groom's family liable to a lawsuit.[2]

Understanding the importance of the wedding celebration and the severity of the problem in John 2 helps us understand Mary's concern, as well as Jesus' lack of concern. Jesus understood that the social offence that distressed his mother paled in comparison to his heavenly priorities. Nevertheless, he used this venue to initiate his public ministry and performed his first recorded miracle.

A CLOSER LOOK

Journey back for a moment to a first-century wedding feast. Jesus attends the wedding in Cana of Galilee three days after calling Philip and Nathanael as disciples (John 1:43–51; 2:1). It's unclear why Jesus and his disciples attend; they may have been invited because Mary is involved in the wedding. More likely, they owe their invitation to Nathanael, a native of Cana and a recent addition to Jesus' cohort (John 21:2).

> **Quick Bit:** Jesus is not being disrespectful to Mary here. He uses the term "woman" (*gynai*) as a polite address to the women he encounters throughout John's Gospel (John 4:21; 8:10; 20:15). He also uses the term from the cross when addressing Mary in a loving, caring way (John 19:26). What's significant in Jesus' statement is that he doesn't share Mary's concern. His concerns are dictated by the Father's will, and they don't include a lack of wine.

When the host of the festivities runs out of wine, Mary informs Jesus of the predicament. Since at this point Jesus hasn't performed any miracles, it's unlikely that Mary is asking for one now. She probably just wants his input. But Jesus reveals a surprising lack of concern, stating, "What does your concern have to do with me, woman? My hour has not yet come" (John 2:4).

In John's Gospel, Jesus' allusions to his "hour" refer to his passion—his death, resurrection, and ascension (John 7:30; 8:20; 12:23, 27; 13:1; 17:1). His use of the term here signals a shift in his thinking as his mind turns toward Jerusalem—toward fulfilling the purpose he came to earth to achieve: redemption. This focus trumps the concerns of his mother and the wedding host.

Mary seems to pick up on Jesus' meaning, and she no doubt senses something different about her son. His focus is changing. Her response to the servants indicates both confusion and anticipation: "Whatever he says to you, do it!" (John 2:5). Jesus says that he isn't concerned about the wine, but he also mentions "his time." Perhaps Mary anticipates that this is the beginning of Jesus' messianic ministry—that he will take this opportunity to reveal himself as Messiah (John 2:11).

Although the time for his passion hasn't arrived, the time to begin his ministry in earnest has. Jesus commands the servants to fetch roughly 180 gallons of water to fill six jars. Given the primitive means of drawing water—collecting it in buckets from a well—this would take a considerable amount of time. When the servants complete their task, Jesus simply says, "Now draw some out and take it to the head steward" (John 2:8).

Surprisingly, Jesus doesn't receive much attention for the miracle. Although the servants know where the wine came from, they apparently keep that fact to themselves, as the head steward remains oblivious (John 2:9). As the festivities continue, Jesus quietly slips into the background—a surprising move for a prophet making his debut.

But Jesus' first recorded miracle isn't meant to convince the masses. It is intended to confirm his disciples' suspicions about Jesus' identity from their previous interactions. In John 1 they followed Jesus and identified him as Israel's Messiah (John 1:35-37, 41, 45, 49). The sign that he performs at Cana confirms that God is with him. By the time they leave Cana, the disciples are truly convinced because Jesus has "revealed his glory" to them (John 2:11).

This initial shift in Jesus' ministry is subtle but definite. It marks a transition in his relationships. As his ministry gets under way, he gathers disciples to himself. His statement in John 2:4 signals a change in priorities: His focus is no longer on matters that might concern a firstborn son, but on his heavenly Father's program of redemption. With this program initiated, Jesus leaves with his mother, brothers, and disciples—all apparently still on good terms (John 2:12).

By the time we reach the incident in Mark's Gospel, however, a rift has developed between Jesus and his family. After Jesus returns home from some of his early evangelistic work, a great crowd follows him and clamors to see him. Apparently, those who knew Jesus before the start of his ministry think that he is out of his mind, and they appeal to his family to rein him in. His family complies with this request, showing that they do not fully understand him.

Quick Bit: The Gospel of Mark doesn't explicitly say that Mary is part of "the family" that goes out to restrain Jesus. In Mark 3:21, the Greek phrase *hoi par' autou* ("those from beside him") may be an ambiguous reference to Jesus' relatives, disciples, or townsfolk. Alternatively, the phrase—commonly translated as "family"—is used to refer to parents and close relatives in other Greek writings of the period. Although it may refer to people Jesus knew in his village before his messianic ministry, Mark may be using the phrase to make a pun, referring to Jesus' mother and brothers in *both* Mark 3:21 and 3:31. If so, the townspeople appeal to Jesus' family ("those from beside him") in Mark 3:21 because they think Jesus is insane ("outside of himself"; *exeste*). His family's attempt to restrain him would have therefore been ironic: those who knew him best misunderstood him.

Mary's role in all of this is uncertain. Throughout the Gospels, she's regularly portrayed as a passive observer, whereas Jesus' brothers are portrayed as aggressors who are antagonistic to his ministry (see John 7:5). Mary is likely included in this confrontation to be a calming, convincing presence: Perhaps Jesus will listen to his mother. The arrival of the scribes from Jerusalem and their accusations against Jesus only escalate the situation. Blasphemers and sorcerers—which the scribes accuse Jesus of being in Mark 3:22—were subject to the death penalty (Lev 20:27; 24:16). By this point, Mary has grasped that her son's mission will place him in harm's way. Yet she also knows what it is like to be the victim of community scorn. As the whisperings and accusations against her son grow more pronounced and dangerous, we can imagine that Mary's desire to protect him becomes overpowering. Mary is likely trying to save her son and avoid further conflict.

After describing the brief encounter with the scribes, Mark resumes the narrative from Mark 3:21. Jesus' family comes to him and requests an audience. At this point, the rift between Jesus and his family widens, and he redefines who his family is: "For whoever does the will of God, this person is my brother and sister and mother" (Mark 3:35). Jesus loves his family, but he desires that they obey God first and follow him. They don't in this episode, which he doesn't condemn them for, but they eventually come to understand him to be Israel's Messiah after his resurrection (Acts 1:14).

Unfortunately, Jesus' relationships—at least with his brothers—are temporarily affected during his ministry. Jesus is forced to sacrifice these relationships for the sake of achieving God's plan. As Mary watches her family rip apart, she must feel torn herself. Could this rift really be part of God's will? Yet this is just one of the many sacrifices that she will be required to make as she devotedly follows God's plan for herself and her son. Although she doesn't understand the full scope of what God is doing, she appears eventually to accept Jesus' foreordained role. Her presence at the cross and her inclusion among his female followers from Galilee indicate that she becomes a disciple before he dies (John 19:25). There, her sacrifice includes a redefinition of her role: Priority is given to her identity as a disciple of Christ and servant of God, and not to her status as Jesus' mother.

Both of these incidents communicate the palpable tensions between Jesus and those who knew him before his public ministry. They also demonstrate the radical sacrifices that were necessary to bring about the salvation of humanity. Mary and Jesus remain devoted to that plan, but they experience it in different ways. Jesus' sacrifice results in a temporary estrangement from his family, while Mary's means the loss of her son.

THROUGHOUT THE BIBLE

The Bible teaches us that sacrifice is required as part of our relationship with God. This shouldn't surprise us since God himself made the greatest sacrifice of all: sending his Son to die for our sins and provide us with eternal life (John 3:16–17). Jesus maintained this perspective throughout his ministry. He was aware that his sacrificial death was the objective of his life (Mark 9:31). He was equally aware that the journey to the cross would be accompanied by misunderstanding and estrangement.

As the Messiah, Jesus lived in a way that was difficult for those around him to comprehend. The more he grew into his role, the more his priorities changed. These changes were especially difficult for his family to understand. At best, they called him radical; at worst, insane (Mark 3:21). He was forced to sacrifice some of these relationships to bring about the redemption of humanity.

We see this motif of familial loss for the sake of salvation throughout the OT. God designated Joseph from an early age as the means by which he would preserve the young nation of Israel (Gen 37:5–12). Joseph's brothers misunderstood this and became jealous, eventually selling him into slavery (Gen 37:25-28). But God brought Joseph to Egypt and used him to sustain his family during a devastating seven-year famine. Once their wickedness was uncovered, Joseph's brothers feared reprisals. But Joseph credited God's sovereignty: "As for you, you planned evil against me, but God planned it for good, in order to do this—to keep many people alive—as it is today" (Gen 50:20). God used their initial misunderstanding to bring about salvation.

David also experienced family discord. He went from being the least of eight brothers to Israel's anointed king (1 Sam 16:6-13). When the Philistine army lined up for battle against Israel, David brought provisions to his brothers' troop, dutifully serving his father and brothers while he waited for God to establish his throne. When Eliab, his oldest brother, heard David asking about Goliath, he rebuked him: "Why have you come down today, and with whom have you left those few sheep in the wilderness? I know your presumptuousness and the evil of your heart! For you have come down in order to see the battle!" (1 Sam 17:28). But David's motives were pure, and God used him that day to kill Goliath and end the Philistine threat against Israel. God brought about a mighty deliverance through David—something that his brothers didn't understand until later (1 Sam 22:1-2).

Although Jesus valued family, he valued obedience to God's will even more. This meant sacrificing familial relationships to remain faithful to God's plan for redemption. His family attempted to restrain him during his ministry (Mark 3:21, 31); they wouldn't understand his true role until after his resurrection (Acts 1:14).

Jesus' redefinition of family must have been painful for Mary. Change is never easy to endure, and family conflicts are the worst of changes. Yet she also recognized that Jesus wasn't an ordinary member of her family: He was God's Son, and he was destined to bring salvation to the world. Mary's devotion to God's plan meant embracing the future that Gabriel had announced (Matt 1:21; Luke 1:31-33). Recognizing that Jesus' destiny was of the utmost importance, Mary gracefully surrendered her role as his mother and stepped into the new role of devoted follower—following her son even to the cross (John 19:25-27).

BEYOND THE BIBLE

Jesus' shocking statements about family relations often appear contra-
dictory to his message of love (compare Matt 10:34–38 and Matt 22:36–40).
But the exact opposite is true. Inherent in these statements is the concept
of radical love and devotion: We must be so dedicated to God that love for
family pales in comparison.

> **Quick Bit:** Theodore of Mopsuestia was an influential scholar in the
> early church. He was a champion of the Antioch school of interpre-
> tation, a school known for interpreting the Bible literally. He served
> as bishop of Mopsuestia (Yakapinar in modern day Turkey) from
> AD 392–428.

Not that Jesus didn't love his immediate family; his thinking about Mary's
well-being while he hung on the cross shows that he cared deeply for his
mother (John 19:26–27). But when his mother and brothers sought to de-
tain him (Mark 3:21, 31–35), he redefined "family" as those who do God's
will. Theodore of Mopsuestia (ca. AD 350–428), a famous interpreter of
Scripture, reflected on this passage and wrote: "For just as he himself
says to the disciples, 'he who loves father or mother more than me is not
worthy of me,' in the same way, I think, Jesus sets a higher value on his
disciples than on his 'mother and brothers.' "[3]

For Jesus, obedience to God, the heavenly Father, is the hallmark of true
kinship. Theodore made a similar connection: "[Jesus] said these things,
not in contempt of his mother and his brothers, but in order to show that
he values more highly closeness of soul than any blood relation of body."[4]
Jesus' concern was that people obey God, even if their families considered
them "crazy." And this wasn't merely a preaching point for Jesus; the eth-
ic carried over into his own family life. He was willing to sacrifice those
relationships for the sake of doing the Father's will.

At times, radical love and devotion result in estrangement from family. Jesus said that his followers must be willing to make this sacrifice
(Matt 10:37–38), and he knew its reality all too well (John 7:5). For Mary,
Jesus' decision meant accepting that God's purpose for him was more important than their mother-son relationship. Part of her devotion to God's

plan would include relinquishing her son to God's purposes so that the world could know his love.

APPLICATION

Although Jesus loved his family, they were ultimately incorporated into the broader category of "disciples." Jesus' mission was about something bigger than sonship or brotherhood; it was about *the* Sonship, his submission to his heavenly Father, and *the* Brotherhood, the Church.

No one felt this separation more intensely than Jesus' own mother, but no one embraced it more fully either. Mary watched her child grow and mature not just as a man, but as a prophet. She observed the shifts that took place in his development: He transitioned from being a son under her care to the Son of God carrying out his plan of redemption. Jesus' assertions in these two stories did more than communicate his mission—they marked a change in authority. Rather than listening to his mother or brothers, Jesus was committed to carrying out God's desires. So Mary moved to the background as the cross came to the fore. Part of her unique role in Jesus' life would be to let go of her son, allowing God to have his way with him. The plan all along was redemption, and Mary knew that (Luke 1:31–33). What she discovered in these events was how much it would hurt (Luke 2:34–35).

On several occasions Jesus mentioned his forthcoming passion (the "hour" in John's Gospel; see John 2:4). This was the impetus for his redefinition of family. His destiny was about suffering for the sake of humanity. And since he knew what was coming, he called his disciples to walk in his steps. His concern was about obedience to the Father's will—a concern his followers had to share. God's will for Mary included giving up her son to him and following the example he set. She accepted this role and became the model for discipleship.

These stories teach us that Jesus' focus should be our focus. Although we may not be facing the cross, we should be willing to (Luke 9:23). When God asks difficult things of us, we should respond the way Jesus and Mary did. And like Mary, we need to be willing to give up everything in perfect obedience, even when it's the most difficult thing we've ever had to do.

DISCUSSION

A Closer Look

1. How can understanding Jesus' priorities help us to correct our own?

_____

_____

_____

2. Have you had to sacrifice relationships in your walk with the Christ? How has God used this in your life to achieve his purposes?

_____

_____

_____

Throughout the Bible

1. How is sacrifice understood in relation to discipleship?

_____

_____

_____

2. How can Mary's transition from mother to disciple serve as a model for us?

_____

_____

_____

Beyond the Bible

1. Read Matthew 10:37-38. How do you understand Jesus' statement here? How does Jesus' life illustrate these verses?

_____

_____

_____

2. What sacrifices have you made to follow Christ? What else would you be willing to sacrifice?

_____

_____

_____

Application

1. What can you do to more fully dedicate yourself to God's will?

_____

_____

_____

2. What steps can you take to ensure that your focus aligns with Jesus'?

_____

_____

_____

CHAPTER 8

BEHOLD YOUR SON

Read John 19:25–27.

SETTING THE STAGE

Theme. We've all been affected by Christ's sacrifice on the cross. Chances are we've spent time meditating on the suffering he experienced for our sake. Perhaps we have looked to his example to help us withstand ridicule or rejection in our own lives. But rarely do we consider how Jesus' death on the cross affected those closest to him.

Mary experienced her son's sacrifice firsthand. She stood watch as her oldest child died a slow, shameful death. Crucifixion was a death penalty reserved for criminals, and the shame of seeing Jesus pierced on the cross would surely have pierced Mary's own soul, just as Simeon had predicted (Luke 2:35). Mary, who had been devoted to God's plan since she was young, already recognized that God's mission for Jesus meant she would have to let him go. Now, God's plan required her to watch him die.

Literary Context. The account of Christ's death on the cross occurs near the end of all four Gospels. His crucifixion was the culmination of his work on earth and the purpose for his coming. Jesus alluded to his eventual death several times throughout his ministry. For example, all three Synoptic Gospels describe Jesus telling his disciples about his death on three separate occasions.[1] Yet in these situations the disciples failed to understand or were distressed by what Jesus said. Peter even went so far as to rebuke him (Matt 16:22; Mark 8:32).

Quick Bit: It is unclear exactly whom Matthew and Mark are referring to when they mention "Mary the mother of James and Joseph"[2] (Matt 27:56; Mark 15:40). Jesus had brothers named James and Joseph (Matt 13:55; Mark 6:3), so the Gospel writers could be referring to Jesus' mother here. However, it is strange that Matthew and Mark do not identify her as "Mary the mother of Jesus." They may instead be referring to "Mary the wife of Clopas" described in John 19:25.

It is unclear whether Mary was aware that Jesus told others about his impending death. Shortly after Jesus' birth, Simeon told her that "a sword will pierce your own soul" (Luke 2:35). While this was probably an allusion to Jesus' death, we don't know whether Mary understood the message in this way (see Chapter 4). Like the disciples, she likely failed to completely grasp God's purpose for her son. The Gospel writers, especially Luke, describe her pondering the many unusual events surrounding her son (Luke 2:19, 51). We know from Gabriel's pronouncement and Elizabeth's blessing (Luke 1:31-33; 42-46) that Mary understood her baby would change the world, but from her interactions with him, we can see that she did not fully comprehend his purpose or the details of God's plan for him (Mark 3:31-35; John 2:4).

Despite her inability to understand the enormity of God's purpose for her son, Mary remained devoted. At the very end of Jesus' life, after most of his disciples had fled, Mary was present at the cross. Only John mentions Mary specifically (John 19:25). Luke may have included her among "the women" (Luke 23:49), and Matthew and Mark may refer to her when they mention "Mary the mother of James and Joseph" (Matt 27:56; Mark 15:40). Regardless of the ambiguity in the Synoptic Gospels, Mary's presence at the cross is clear in John's Gospel: Even as he hung on the cross, Jesus ensured that she would be cared for after his death (John 19:26-27).

Historical & Cultural Background. Mary's experience at the cross— watching her son die a humiliating and excruciating death—must have been agonizing. Crucifixion was a public method of torture and execution reserved for criminals. Although the Persians and Greeks used it before them, the Romans popularized the use of crucifixion as punishment for rebels and fugitive slaves—sometimes crucifying a large number of people at once. The criminal's offense was often written on a tablet that he would be forced to carry or wear around his neck.

The Jewish historian Josephus described crucifixion as "a most miserable death" (*The Jewish War* 7 §203). Before being crucified, the victim would typically be flogged or beaten. He would then have to carry the crossbeam to the place of crucifixion. The victim would be nailed or tied to the crossbeam, which would then be fixed to a stake driven into the ground. Then the victim's feet would be nailed or bound to the vertical stake. Death came slowly as the person's position on the cross made every breath a searing struggle. In certain cases, guards would break the victim's legs to hasten death.

The entire process of crucifixion—from flogging to eventual death—was meant to inflict shame as well as pain. Mary would have been tormented to see her son die in such a way. Like any mother, she would have felt great shame and disgrace at seeing him die a criminal's death, her grief amplified by knowing he was innocent. Surely this was not the end she had expected when Gabriel told her that she would give birth to a child who would "reign over the house of Jacob forever" (Luke 1:32-33). However, as Mary had seen already, God's plan rarely aligns with our expectations.

A CLOSER LOOK

Imagine Mary's experience that day. The devastation of Jesus' crucifixion dismantles her understanding of her entire life experience. Although it's unclear whether Mary fully understood that Jesus was destined to die so that others may live (see John 12:27-36), nothing can prepare a mother for witnessing the death of her child, not even that great hope. It's in this moment of deep despair that Jesus tells John to care for Mary—"Behold your mother" (John 19:27; see Mark 3:24; see Chapter 7)—furthering his earlier idea that Mary and John are part of one large spiritual family.

We can only wonder how Mary bears her grief as she watches her son beaten and mocked (John 19:1-3). The sorrow and shame must be overwhelming as the crowd—led by the religious leaders—chants "Crucify him! Crucify him!" (John 19:6, 15), and the soldiers taunt him and divide his clothing (Luke 23:36; John 19:23-24).

Like any mother, Mary must ache to rescue her son. She is helpless to alter the situation, crippled by what she witnesses. Mary has already relinquished her son to his Father's divine purpose. She has seen him teach in the temple, perform miracles, and redefine his family as those who obey the will of God (Mark 3:35). Now she watches as he fulfills his Father's ultimate will (Matt 26:39). But while Mary is powerless to help him, Jesus can and does reach out to help her.

Mary is most likely a widow by the time Jesus is crucified. The Gospels do not mention Joseph, her husband, after the story of the 12-year-old Jesus at the temple (see Chapter 6). Jesus was probably about 30 years old when he began his public ministry, which lasted three years. This would mean that Mary—who was in her early to mid-teens when Jesus was born (see Chapter 1)—is most likely in her late 40s at the time of Jesus' death. It is unlikely that Joseph—probably 10 to 15 years older than Mary—is still alive.

In Jewish families, the oldest son was responsible for providing for his widowed mother. Mary may have been following Jesus during the final part of his ministry and relying on him for support. If so, his death would leave her without any means of provision. The Gospels do not say where Jesus' brothers are at this point. Earlier, they demonstrated their unbelief in Jesus (John 7:5), but they would later be counted among his disciples (Acts 1:14).[3]

Jesus shows his care and concern for his mother by using one of his final breaths to make sure she is not abandoned. He says to John, "Behold your mother," and to Mary, "Woman, behold your son" (John 19:26–27). With these words, Jesus transfers the responsibility of Mary's care to John, "the disciple whom he loved." Even as he is giving his life for her (and our) spiritual needs, he ensures that her physical needs are met.

> **Quick Bit:** Throughout the Gospel of John, the author refers to a disciple "whom Jesus loved" (John 13:23).[4] There are several possibilities as to the identity of this disciple. The phrase might refer to Lazarus, whom John elsewhere identifies as someone whom Jesus loves (John 11:3, 5, 36). However, the disciple "whom Jesus loved" is closely associated with Peter in John's Gospel, and Lazarus is not associated with Peter elsewhere. Most likely, the disciple "whom Jesus loved" is John, the son of Zebedee (Mark 1:19). John and Peter are closely

associated elsewhere (Luke 22:8; Acts 3:1), just as they are in John's Gospel (John 20:2; 21:20). Also, John is never mentioned by name in the Gospel of John.

Jesus' statement in John 19:26–27 is one of only seven he makes while on the cross. Luke records Jesus' first two statements: "Father, forgive them, for they do not know what they are doing" (Luke 23:34) and "Truly I say to you, today you will be with me in paradise" (Luke 23:43). Both statements show the grace and forgiveness Christ displays on the cross. Even while dying, Jesus shows compassion toward those who are crucifying him and to one of the criminals dying alongside him.

After he speaks to his mother and John, Jesus speaks to the completion of his work on earth. John records him saying "I thirst" as a fulfillment of Scripture (John 19:28). Matthew and Mark record him quoting Psalm 22:1: "My God, my God, why have you forsaken me?" (Matt 27:46; Mark 15:34). Luke records Jesus dedicating himself one final time to his Father's will with a quotation from Psalm 31:5 (see Luke 23:46). Finally, John records Jesus' acknowledgement that his work on earth is done when he speaks for the last time: "It is finished" (John 19:30 ESV).[5]

Mary is an eyewitness to her son's suffering and death—and to the amazing compassion and grace he displays on the cross. His forgiving response to the crowd's taunts were an example to her and all those present, just as it is to us today. She also sees Jesus' compassion and grace extend directly to her, as he, in the midst of his suffering, ensures that she is not forgotten.

No matter how deep, Mary's grief at losing her son is temporary. Christ's death is not permanent—he is resurrected on the third day. The Gospels do not record Mary interacting with Jesus after his resurrection. However, in Acts we see Mary, along with her other sons, working with Jesus' disciples after his ascension (Acts 1:13–14). As a young woman, Mary devoted herself to God's plan, humbly declaring herself "the servant of the Lord" (Luke 1:38 ESV). Now that God's purpose for her son is accomplished, Mary continues her faithful devotion to God's plan, now as one of Jesus' disciples.

THROUGHOUT THE BIBLE

At this difficult time, Mary could have taken comfort in the hope of Jesus' promised resurrection (Matt 16:21-23; 17:22-23; compare John 11:17-27); but like the rest of the disciples, Mary didn't yet understand the reason for his death. As John tells us directly, "they did not yet know the scripture, that it was necessary for him [Jesus] to rise from the dead" (John 20:9).

However, OT prophecy could have provided hope for Mary. More than 500 years before Jesus' birth, Isaiah 53:10 told of a Suffering Servant who would "prolong days," "see his offspring," and "see light" after his death as a "guilt offering."[6] Jesus fulfilled this prophecy.[7] Jesus' death and burial mirrors the depiction of the Suffering Servant in Isaiah 52:13–53:12.[8] In addition, Jesus' life and death fits the description of the lamenter's suffering in Psalm 22.[9] If Mary and the other disciples had recognized the prophetic parallels to Jesus' life, they might have perceived his death differently. They might have understood it as a beginning rather than an end.

> **Quick Bit:** Demonstrating Jesus' fulfillment of prophecy (see Isa 52:13–53:12; Psa 22), Luke's Gospel tells us that after his resurrection, Jesus "beginning from Moses and from all the prophets ... interpreted to [the two men Jesus met on the road to Emmaus] the things concerning himself in all the scriptures" (Luke 24:27). This is also why, when Jesus commissioned his disciples, he said, "These are my words that I spoke to you while I was still with you, that everything that is written about me in the law of Moses and the prophets and psalms must be fulfilled" (Luke 24:44).

Nonetheless, Mary remained visible in the final events of her son's life and was part of the community that emerged out of his resurrection. She remained at the foot of the cross as Christ died, and she later visited his tomb—actions that showed great courage on her part given Jesus' status as a criminal under Roman law. She was probably with the disciples when they first learned that Jesus had risen, and she was present as the post-resurrection Church developed. Luke tells us in Acts that "All these [male disciples of Jesus] were busily engaged with one mind in prayer, together with the women and Mary the mother of Jesus and with his brothers" (Acts 1:14). Mary's continued devotion gave her a place in Jesus' ongoing spiritual family, and thus a major role in the Church at large.

Quick Bit: Luke's note in Acts about Mary and the other women being present isn't merely an acknowledgment of her and the others (Acts 1:14); it reflects a fundamental cultural shift. The early church included men and women together—a unity of worshipers that was uncommon in the first century AD.

In light of the larger prophetic framework around Jesus' death and resurrection, Mary can be viewed as having merely played a small role in this drama. But Jesus' deep concern for her from the cross indicates that her presence provided him with comfort as he suffered. In the midst of such desperation, we see not only the light of resurrection on the other side of Jesus' life, but the light of one who followed him to his very death at great personal risk and cost. In that moment, we see a mother and her grown son—and yet we also see that mother become one of Jesus' first disciples. As Jesus became everything he was meant to be, Mary became everything she was meant to be: an integral part of God's unfolding story of the redemption of humanity and a model of devotion to God's ultimate plan.

BEYOND THE BIBLE

Mary endured every parent's worst nightmare: watching her child die. After more than 30 years, Simeon's ominous words from Luke 2:34–35 became a reality. Mary's long-anticipated, sword-like grief coincided with her vision of Jesus' nail-pierced hands. He was betrayed by his own people, shamefully executed as a criminal, and nailed to a Roman cross. Yet in their anguish, Mary and Jesus were united: Mary faithfully obeyed God by giving up her son, and Jesus faithfully obeyed his Father by giving up his life.

Mary's suffering resembles that of another mother from Jewish history. The book of 2 Maccabees tells the story of a devout mother and her seven sons who refused the Greek king Antiochus IV Epiphanes' order to eat the flesh of swine, a direct violation of Deuteronomy 14:8. The king's goal was to eliminate Jewish distinctions, such as dietary laws, and thus dilute Israelite identity so that the people would abandon their God and be incorporated in Greek life. Death awaited those who disobeyed the king's directive.

Quick Bit: Second Maccabees recounts the suffering of the Jews under the reign of the Greek tyrant Antiochus IV Epiphanes and their subsequent revolt under the leadership of Judas Maccabeus. Although it is not included in Protestant Bibles, it is part of the Roman Catholic and Eastern Orthodox traditions.

When the brothers refused the evil king, Antiochus tortured them while their mother watched. The brothers suffered a variety torments: being scalped, boiled, fried, having their hands and feet cut off, and having their tongues removed. The king piled their bodies close to their mother one by one, hoping that she would persuade each successive son to eat the swine and abandon his faith—but she did not, and all died rather than submit. The text tells of her grief and their valor: "O mother, tried now by more bitter pains than even the birth pangs you suffered for them! O woman, who alone gave birth to such complete devotion!" (4 Macc 15:16–17 NRSV).[10]

Her own speech during this experience is even more remarkable. Rather than pleading with her sons to compromise their faith and violate God's law, she encouraged them to embrace their role—even when faced with death:

> She encouraged each of them in the language of their ancestors. Filled with a noble spirit, she ... said to them, "I do not know how you came into being in my womb. It was not I who gave you life and breath, nor I who set in order the elements within each of you. Therefore the Creator of the world, who shaped the beginning of humankind and devised the origin of all things, will in his mercy give life and breath back to you again, since you now forget yourselves for the sake of his laws" (2 Macc 7:20–23 NRSV).

Like these seven sons, Jesus was willing to forsake himself for God's plan. Mary also was willing to forsake herself—body and soul—so that God might accomplish his plan of redemption through her. Words can't express the anguish Mary must have felt at the foot of the cross (John 19:25), but she embodied the definition of discipleship: "The one who loves son or daughter more than me is not worthy of me. And whoever does not take up his cross and follow me is not worthy of me" (Matt 10:37–38). Mary was devoted to God's plan, and she was willing to give up everything—even her son—to see it fulfilled.

APPLICATION

Every life brings loss. As children, we may be devastated when best friends move away or a favorite pet dies. As adults, we grieve when those we love are injured or killed in accidents, when cancer claims a colleague, or when our parents or siblings die. Losses come in all forms and all degrees, and death is a natural consequence of life. But arguably the most painful loss is when a parent must bury a child, no matter their age, because it defies our definition of natural order. Mary had likely already lost her husband. Now she stood at the foot of the cross, risking her life to watch her firstborn son die a criminal's death.

Mary knew loss, and she was no stranger to shame, having been an unwed teenage mother under divine but dubious circumstances. Throughout her life Mary surrendered herself to be God's servant, making one painful sacrifice after another in her devotion to God and his plan for her to be the mother of his Son. As she watched him hang on the cross in torment, surrounded by a hostile crowd and Roman guards, she must have agonized. She knew from the time Jesus was a toddler that his life was in danger, but when Gabriel said God would give her a son that would be King, she would not have imagined him dying a criminal's death. As the soldiers pierced his side with the sword, Simeon's words—"a sword will pierce through your own soul also" (Luke 2:35)—must have echoed in her heart. Even if she was aware of the prophecy of the Suffering Servant in Isaiah, in this moment, gripped by sorrow, grief, loneliness, and uncertainty, Mary must have wondered how God's plan would move forward from Golgotha.

When Jesus called out to John, "Behold your mother," and to Mary, "Behold your son" (John 19:26–27), he fulfilled his responsibility as the firstborn son to make sure Mary was cared for the rest of her life. In doing so, he established the new vision of family he spoke of, a family of those who follow him. In the same moment, he made provision for Mary's spiritual care—and ours. From Jesus' conception to his death on the cross and into a life of discipleship after his resurrection, Mary remained humbly devoted to God's plan, no matter the cost.

DISCUSSION

A Closer Look

1. Reflect on Christ's sacrifice on the cross. Does thinking about this event from Mary's perspective give you more insight into Jesus' suffering? In what ways?

_____

_____

_____

2. What do Jesus' statements from the cross tell you about his priorities? How can you display a Christ-like compassion and forgiveness in your life?

_____

_____

_____

Throughout the Bible

1. Read Isaiah 52:13–53:12. How does this passage help you understand Christ's work of salvation on the cross?

_____

_____

_____

2. Read Psalm 22. How does the suffering of the psalmist compare with Christ's suffering? Hoes does the ending of that psalm (Psa 22:22–31) encourage you to celebrate Christ's resurrection?

_____

_____

_____

Beyond the Bible

1. Have you had to make sacrifices as you devotedly follow God? If so, what are they? If not, are you willing to make such sacrifices?

_____

_____

_____

2. In what ways have you benefited from Mary's devotion to God's plan?

_____

_____

_____

Application

1. If you had been alive to follow Jesus in his ministry, not knowing he would rise again, what emotions would you have felt when he died? Would you have taken the risk to be there at the cross?

_____

_____

_____

2. Think about a time you experienced a great loss. Were you able to persevere in faith? How?

_____

_____

_____

_____

CONCLUSION

No one could have expected God to choose a young girl from a humble village to play such a pivotal role in his story of redemption. Yet Mary is often overlooked. When considering the Gospels, we usually turn our attention to Jesus' miracles, the elements of his teaching, or the story of his passion. Yet, as we've seen, Mary remained a courageous and loving presence throughout the story of her son, whether in the foreground or the background of the narratives.

Like all mothers, Mary cared deeply for her son and desired the best for him, in his youth and his adulthood. She anchored Jesus in his humanity while simultaneously bearing witness to his divinity. Mary embodied the essence of motherhood, discipleship, and the gospel of grace. Few characters in the history of salvation were asked to relinquish as much as she did.

Mary's role in God's plan of redemption is best understood when considering her relationship to another important woman in the biblical narrative: Eve. Genesis tells us that Eve fell victim to the serpent's deception, initiating the deadly affliction of sin that affected all subsequent generations, severing humanity from its Creator. In his loving-kindness, God chose Mary to bear the Savior, Jesus, whose death on the cross cured us and restored our relationship to the One whose love surpasses all understanding. Irenaeus (ca. AD 130–200), an influential thinker in the early church, famously remarked, "The knot of Eve's disobedience was untied by Mary's obedience; for what Eve bound by her unbelief, Mary loosed by her faith."[1] Mary, in contrast to her ancient ancestor, devoted herself to God's desires and acted with the faith necessary to carry out his plan.

Throughout the story of redemption, God used ordinary men and women: Noah, Abraham, Joseph, Moses, David, Esther, and others. But Mary represents the culmination of God's redemptive efforts. Through her came Israel's long-awaited redeemer, the Messiah, who would "save his people from their sins" (Matt 1:21). This good news of God's grace came first to Mary and was made manifest through her to all generations that followed.

Just as God freely chose to extend his grace to us through the radical event of the incarnation, Mary freely chose to participate as the Lord's "handmaiden," accepting the role of "servant" (Luke 1:38). In that moment of assent, Mary willingly became a vessel for Christ's incarnation—God's becoming human—a mystery that believers continue to reflect upon today as an unfathomable well of God's love for us.

Although Jesus' disciples have grown in number from 12 to millions around the world today, Mary's relationship with her son was even more intimate. She alone transitioned from mother of God to child of God. In the latter part of Jesus' ministry, she became the like-minded follower of God that her son wanted her and other believers to be—concerned only with obedience to the Father's will. The journey of her life—through joy, sorrow, sacrifice, and devotion—shows her to be God's image bearer, a model for other followers of Jesus then and now. Mary earnestly gave everything, including her son, to see God's salvation carried out. Her life inspires us to follow a similar path, to be wholly devoted to God's plan.

NOTES

Chapter 1

1. When Elizabeth eventually gives birth to John, Luke portrays it as a time of rejoicing (see Luke 1:57-58).
2. Joseph A. Fitzmyer, *The Gospel According to Luke I-IX: Introduction, Translation, and Notes*, Anchor Yale Bible, vol. 28 (New Haven; London: Yale University Press, 2008), 343.
3. Arthur Just Jr., *New Testament 3: Luke*, Ancient Christian Commentary on Scripture (Downers Grove, IL: IVP Academic, 2005), 15-16.
4. Ibid.

Chapter 2

1. Norval Geldenhuys, *Commentary on the Gospel of Luke: The English Text with Introduction, Exposition and Notes*, The New International Commentary on the Old and New Testament (Grand Rapids, MI: Eerdmans, 1952), 82.
2. If Mary had the higher social standing, Elizabeth would have left her house to initiate the greeting.
3. Joel B. Green, *The Gospel of Luke*, The New International Commentary on the New Testament (Grand Rapids, MI: Eerdmans, 1997), 98-99.
4. Quotations in "Beyond the Bible" adapted from Montague Rhodes James, ed., *The Apocryphal New Testament: Being the Apocryphal Gospels, Acts, Epistles, and Apocalypses* (Oxford: Clarendon Press, 1924), 38-49.

Chapter 3

1. Josephus, *Antiquities* 18.1-2.
2. The Gospels of Luke and Matthew place Jesus' birth during Herod's reign over Judaea (Matt 2:1; Luke 1:5).
3. Although this meaning of *prōtos* is not common, it can be seen in John 1:15 and 15:18.
4. Darrell L. Bock, *Luke Volume 1: 1:1-9:50*, Baker Exegetical Commentary on the New Testament (Grand Rapids, MI: Baker Academic, 1994), 213-14.

5. Ibid., 222.

6. Arthur Just Jr., *New Testament 3: Luke*, Ancient Christian Commentary on Scripture (Downers Grove, IL: IVP Academic, 2005), 24.

7. Ibid., 15.

Chapter 4

1. All OT quotations in this section are from *The Holy Bible: New Revised Standard Version* (Nashville: Thomas Nelson Publishers, 1989).

2. Arthur Just Jr., *New Testament 3: Luke*, Ancient Christian Commentary on Scripture (Downers Grove, IL: IVP Academic, 2005), 50.

Chapter 5

1. Mark and John do not include an account of Jesus' birth.

2. David E. Garland, *Reading Matthew: A Literary and Theological Commentary on the First Gospel*, Reading the New Testament Series (Macon, GA: Smyth & Helwys Publishing, 2001), 26.

3. David L. Turner, *Matthew*, Baker Exegetical Commentary on the New Testament (Grand Rapids, MI: Baker Academic, 2008), 79.

4. Alexander Walker, trans., "The Gospel of Pseudo-Matthew", in *The Ante-Nicene Fathers, Volume VIII: Fathers of the Third and Fourth Centuries: The Twelve Patriarchs, Excerpts and Epistles, the Clementina, Apocrypha, Decretals, Memoirs of Edessa and Syriac Documents, Remains of the First Ages*, ed. Alexander Roberts, James Donaldson, and A. Cleveland Coxe (Buffalo, NY: Christian Literature Company, 1886), 377.

5. Ibid.

6. William Hone, ed., *The Apocryphal New Testament: Being All the Gospels, Epistles, and Other Pieces Now extant*, (London: William Hone, 1820), 41–42.

7. Ibid., 42.

Chapter 6

1. Darrell L. Bock, *Luke Volume 1: 1:1–9:50*, Baker Exegetical Commentary on the New Testament (Grand Rapids, MI: Baker Academic, 1994), 263.

2. The OT distinguishes between "Passover" and the "Feast of Unleavened Bread." The two feasts were celebrated consecutively, with the Feast of Unleavened Bread occurring the seven days after Passover (see 2 Chr 35:17). These two feasts are listed together in the NT (see Matt 26:17; Luke 22:1).

3. Josephus, *Wars of the Jews*, 2.280. Although this number is probably exaggerated, it indicates that many people traveled to Jerusalem during Passover.

4. Bock, *Luke*, 264.

5. Joel B. Green, *The Gospel of Luke*, The New International Commentary on the New Testament (Grand Rapids, MI: Eerdmans, 1997), 155.

6. Bock, *Luke*, 259.

7. Quotations in this section are adapted from Montague Rhodes James, ed., *The Apocryphal New Testament: Being the Apocryphal Gospels, Acts, Epistles, and Apocalypses* (Oxford: Clarendon Press, 1924), 52.

8. Ibid.

9. Ibid.

10. Ibid.

Chapter 7

1. Gerald L. Borchert, *John 1–11*, The New American Commentary, vol. 25A (Nashville: Broadman & Holman Publishers, 1996), 156.

2. Paul P. Enns, "Weddings," in *Holman Illustrated Bible Dictionary*, ed. Chad Brand, et al. (Nashville: Holman Bible Publishers, 2003), 1664.

3. Manilo Simonetti, *New Testament 1a: Matthew 1–13*, Ancient Christian Commentary on Scripture (Downers Grove, IL: InterVarsity Press, 2001), 262.

4. Ibid.

Chapter 8

1. See Matthew 16:21–23; 17:22–23; 20:17–19; Mark 8:31–33; 9:30–32; 10:32–34; Luke 9:21–22, 43–45; 18:31–34.

2. Mark uses the variant "Joses" instead of "Joseph."

3. Jesus' brother, James, later became one of the leaders of the Jerusalem church. See Acts 12:17; 15:13.

4. See also John 19:26; 20:2; 21:7, 20.

5. This statement is only one word (*tetelestai*) in Greek.

6. John D. Barry, *The Resurrected Servant in Isaiah* (Colorado Springs: Paternoster, 2010; Bellingham, WA: Logos Bible Software, 2010).

7. John D. Barry, "A Resurrected Servant 500 Years before Jesus," *Bible Study Magazine*, March/April 2010, 37–39.

8. For example, compare Luke 22:47–53 and John 21:1–14 with Isaiah 53:3; compare Mark 26:26–46 with Isaiah 53:4; compare John 19:34 with Isaiah 53:5; compare Mark 15:27 and John 19:38–42 with Isaiah 53:9.

9. Compare Matthew 27:46 with Psalm 22:1; compare Psalm 22:18 with John 19:23–24; compare John 19:30 with Psalm 22:31.

10. 4 Maccabees 8–18 retells the story of 2 Maccabees 7 in greater detail.

Conclusion

1. Irenaeus of Lyons, "Irenæus Against Heresies," in *The Ante-Nicene Fathers, Volume I: The Apostolic Fathers with Justin Martyr and Irenaeus*, ed. Alexander Roberts, James Donaldson, and A. Cleveland Coxe (Buffalo, NY: Christian Literature Company, 1885), XXII, 4.

SOURCES

Barry, John D. "A Resurrected Servant 500 Years Before Jesus." *Bible Study Magazine*, March/April 2010, 37-39.

———. *The Resurrected Servant in Isaiah*. Colorado Springs: Paternoster, 2010; Bellingham, WA: Logos Bible Software, 2010.

Bernat, David A. "Circumcision." In *The Eerdmans Dictionary of Early Judaism*, edited by John J. Collins and Daniel C. Harlow, 471-474. Grand Rapids, MI; Cambridge, UK: Eerdmans, 2010.

Blackburn, B. L. "Miracles and Miracle Stories." In *Dictionary of Jesus and the Gospels*, edited by Joel B. Green, Scot McKnight, and I. Howard Marshall, 549-559. Downers Grove, IL: InterVarsity Press, 1992.

Bock, Darrell L. *Luke Volume 1: 1:1-9:50*. Baker Exegetical Commentary on the New Testament. Grand Rapids, MI: Baker Academic, 1994.

Borchert, Gerald L. *John 1-11*. The New American Commentary, vol. 25A. Nashville: Broadman & Holman Publishers, 1996.

———. "The Death of the King (18:1-19:42)." In *John 12-21*, 212-285. The New American Commentary, vol. 25B. Nashville: Broadman & Holman Publishers, 2002.

Bower, R. K. and G. L. Knapp. "Marriage; Marry." In *The International Standard Bible Encyclopedia, Revised*, edited by Geoffrey W. Bromiley, vol. 3, 261-266. Grand Rapids, MI: Eerdmans, 1988.

Caneday, A. B. "Sign." In *Eerdmans Dictionary of the Bible*, edited by David Noel Freedman, Allen C. Myers, and Astrid B. Beck, 1219-1220. Grand Rapids, MI: Eerdmans, 2000.

Carson, D. A. "The Trial and Passion of Jesus (18:1-19:42)." In *The Gospel According to John*, 571-631. The Pillar New Testament Commentary. Leicester, England; Grand Rapids, MI: InterVarsity Press; Eerdmans, 1991.

Drumwright, H. L., Jr. "Crucifixion." In *The Zondervan Encyclopedia of the Bible*, edited by Moisés Silva and Merrill Chapin Tenney, vol. 1, 1106–1108. Grand Rapids, MI: Zondervan, 2009.

Enns, Paul P. "Weddings." In *Holman Illustrated Bible Dictionary*, edited by Chad Brand, et al., 1664. Nashville: Holman Bible Publishers, 2003.

Fitzmyer, Joseph A. *The Gospel According to Luke I–IX: Introduction, Translation, and Notes*. Anchor Yale Bible, vol. 28. New Haven; London: Yale University Press, 2008.

Fournier, Keith, and Lela Gilbert. *The Prayer of Mary: Living the Surrendered Life*. Nashville: Thomas Nelson, 2005.

Garland, David E. *Reading Matthew: A Literary and Theological Commentary on the First Gospel*. Reading the New Testament Series. Macon, GA: Smyth & Helwys Publishing, 2001.

Geldenhuys, Norval. *Commentary on the Gospel of Luke: The English Text with Introduction, Exposition and Notes*. The New International Commentary on the Old and New Testament. Grand Rapids, MI: Eerdmans, 1952.

Green, Joel B. "The Announcement of Jesus' Birth." In *The Gospel of Luke*, 82–92. The New International Commentary on the New Testament. Grand Rapids, MI: Eerdmans, 1997.

Hickem, Catherine. *Heaven in Her Arms: Why God Chose Mary to Raise His Son and What It Means for You*. Nashville: Thomas Nelson, 2012.

Hone, William, ed. *The Apocryphal New Testament: Being All the Gospels, Epistles, and Other Pieces Now Extant*. London: William Hone, 1820.

James, Montague Rhodes, ed. *The Apocryphal New Testament: Being the Apocryphal Gospels, Acts, Epistles, and Apocalypses*. Oxford: Clarendon Press, 1924.

Josephus, Flavius, and William Whiston. *The Works of Josephus: Complete and Unabridged*. Peabody: Hendrickson, 1987.

Just, Arthur, Jr. *New Testament 3: Luke*. Ancient Christian Commentary on Scripture. Downers Grove, IL: IVP Academic, 2005.

Klauck, Hans-Josef. *Apocryphal Gospels: An Introduction*. London; New York: T&T Clark, 2003.

Köstenberger, Andreas J. "The Passion Narrative (18:1–19:42)." In *John*, 502–557. Baker Exegetical Commentary on the New Testament. Grand Rapids, MI: Baker Academic, 2004.

Pomykala, K. E. "Messianism." In *The Eerdmans Dictionary of Early Judaism*, edited by J. J. Collins and D. C. Harlow, 938–42. Grand Rapids, MI; Cambridge, UK: Eerdmans, 2010.

Simonetti, Manilo. *New Testament 1a: Matthew 1–13*. Ancient Christian Commentary on Scripture. Downers Grove, IL: InterVarsity Press, 2001.

Stein, Robert H. "The Meeting of John the Baptist and Jesus (1:39–56)." In *Luke*, 88–95. The New American Commentary, vol. 24. Nashville: Broadman & Holman Publishers, 1992.

Talbert, Charles H. *Reading Luke: A Literary and Theological Commentary on the Third Gospel*. Rev. ed. Reading the New Testament Series. Macon, GA: Smyth & Helwys Publishing, 2002.

The Holy Bible: New Revised Standard Version. Nashville: Thomas Nelson, 1989.

Turner, David L. *Matthew*. Baker Exegetical Commentary on the New Testament. Grand Rapids, MI: Baker Academic, 2008.

Walker, Alexander, trans. "The Gospel of Pseudo-Matthew." In *The Ante-Nicene Fathers, Volume VIII: Fathers of the Third and Fourth Centuries: The Twelve Patriarchs, Excerpts and Epistles, the Clementina, Apocrypha, Decretals, Memoirs of Edessa and Syriac Documents, Remains of the First Ages*, edited by Alexander Roberts, James Donaldson, and A. Cleveland Coxe. Buffalo, NY: Christian Literature Company, 1886.

Wilson, M. R. "Passover." In *The International Standard Bible Encyclopedia, Revised*, edited by Geoffrey W. Bromiley, vol. 2, 675–679. Grand Rapids, MI: Eerdmans, 1988.

Witherington, Ben, III. "Birth of Christ." In *Dictionary of Jesus and the Gospels*, edited by Joel B. Green, Scot McKnight, and I. Howard Marshall, 60–74. Downers Grove, IL: InterVarsity Press, 1992.

About the Editor

Michael R. Grigoni has served as managing editor of Bible Reference at Lexham Press. He is the editor of *Mary: Devoted to God's Plan* and two other Studies in Faithful Living volumes. He holds a Master of Theological Studies from Harvard Divinity School. Previously, Michael has served as a trained hospital chaplain, assisted in pastoring, and led worship for large congregations.

About the Authors

Miles Custis is the author of *The End of the Matter: Understanding the Epilogue of Ecclesiastes*, a Faithlife Study Bible contributing editor, the coauthor of Lexham Bible Guides: Genesis Collection, and the coauthor of *Jacob: Discerning God's Presence* and three other Studies in Faithful Living volumes. He holds a Master of Arts in biblical studies from Trinity Western University.

Douglas Mangum is the editor of the Lexham Bible Guides series and the Lexham Methods Series. He is the coauthor of Lexham Bible Guides: Genesis Collection, *Joseph: Understanding God's Purpose* and three other Studies in Faithful Living volumes. He is a Lexham English Bible editor, a Faithlife Study Bible contributing editor, a regular *Bible Study Magazine* contributor, and a frequently consulted specialist for the *Lexham Bible Dictionary*. In addition, he is a PhD candidate in Near Eastern studies at the University of Free State; he holds a Master of Arts in Hebrew and Semitic studies from the University of Wisconsin–Madison.

Matthew M. Whitehead is the coauthor of *Lexham Bible Guide: Ephesians* and three Studies in Faithful Living volumes. He has also served as a Faithlife Study Bible contributing editor. He assisted with the digitization process for the Discoveries in the Judaean Desert series and worked on the Oxford Hebrew Bible project. Matthew holds an MDiv from Northwest Baptist Seminary and is pursuing an MA in biblical studies at Trinity Western University.

Rebecca Brant is the senior editor for Lexham Press. She develops content for Faithlife Study Bible, *Lexham Bible Dictionary*, and *Bible Study Magazine*. She is a regular contributor to *Bible Study Magazine*.

John D. Barry is the publisher of Lexham Press, general editor of Faithlife Study Bible and *Lexham Bible Dictionary*, and the previous editor-in-chief of *Bible Study Magazine*. He is the author of *The Resurrected Servant in Isaiah* and over 100 articles, as well as the coauthor of *Connect the Testaments: A Daily Devotional with Bible Reading Plan*. John is also the author of Not Your Average Bible Study volumes on Malachi, Colossians, Hebrews, James, and 1 Peter, and the coauthor of a study on 2 Peter–Jude.

Elizabeth Vince is a freelance editor who has developed content for Faithlife Study Bible, *Lexham Bible Dictionary*, *Bible Study Magazine*, and *Connect the Testaments*. She is a regular contributor to *Bible Study Magazine*.